W9-BWF-327

921
FRA
3 24571 0900250 5
Miller, Brandon
Marie.

Benjamin Franklin,
American genius :
his life and ideas,
with 21 activit$10.85

921
FRA
3 24571 0900250 5
Miller, Brandon
Marie.

Benjamin Franklin,
American genius :
his life and ideas,
with 21 activities

Benjamin Franklin

AMERICAN GENIUS

❧ *His Life and Ideas* ❧

with 21 Activities

BRANDON MARIE MILLER

CHICAGO REVIEW PRESS

Library of Congress Cataloging-in-Publication Data

Miller, Brandon Marie.

    Benjamin Franklin, American genius : his life and ideas, with 21 activities / Brandon Marie Miller.

        p. cm.

    Includes bibliographical references.

    ISBN 978-1-55652-757-9 (pbk.)

    1. Franklin, Benjamin, 1706-1790—Juvenile literature. 2. Statesmen—United States—Biography—Juvenile literature. 3. Inventors—United States—Biography—Juvenile literature. 4. Scientists—United States—Biography—Juvenile literature. 5. Printers—United States—Biography—Juvenile literature. 6. Creative activities and seat work—Juvenile literature. 7. Handicraft—Juvenile literature. 8. Cookery—Juvenile literature. 9. Games—Juvenile literature. I. Title.

    E302.6.F8M6544 2009

    973.3092—dc22

    [B]

    2009012456

Cover and interior design: Monica Baziuk

Cover images courtesy of: Benjamin Franklin Institute of Technology, Library of Congress, and Shutterstock

Interior images are reprinted courtesy of the following: Charles Mills Murals, courtesy of Benjamin Franklin Institute of Technology, 41 Berkeley Street, Boston, MA. Photographer: Bahman Zonoozi, pages: 12, 14, 28, 49, 51, 58, 69, 90 / Huntington Library, page 74 / Independence National Historical Park, pages 60, 111 (sidebar) / Janeen Coyle, page 59 / Library of Congress, pages: 13, 18, 19, 23, 34, 35, 39, 45, 47, 52, 57, 64, 67, 68, 75, 80, 81, 84, 86, 87, 89, 91, 93, 94, 95, 98, 99, 100, 106, 107, 108, 111, 114, 115 / North Wind Picture Archives, pages: 2, 21, 27, 82, 110

Published by Chicago Review Press, Incorporated

814 North Franklin Street

Chicago, Illinois 60610

ISBN 978-1-55652-757-9

Printed in the United States of America

5 4 3 2 1

To Mom and Aunt Marty

I miss you

CONTENTS

❧ 1 ❧
"AS A YOUNG GENIUS"—1

ACKNOWLEDGMENTS

MY THANKS to the Chael family for helping to test the activities. Thanks to Paul Miller for supplying the computer expertise I sadly lack. My thanks to Janeen Coyle for visiting Craven Street in London.

My deep appreciation to the Huntington Library, Art Collections, and Botanical Gardens in San Marino, California, for use of the painting *Benjamin Franklin Appearing before the Privy Council* by Christian Schussele.

I'd especially like to mention the Benjamin Franklin Institute of Technology in Boston, which has graciously allowed me to use its 1908 Charles Mills paintings based on Franklin's life. The really fun aspect is that the Institute was founded in part with money bequeathed in Benjamin Franklin's will to aid apprentices in his hometown. This book is much richer thanks to the Institute's generous spirit.

TIME LINE

including 16-month-old Ebenezer, who drowned in the tallow shop's boiling vat. On January 17, 1706, Abiah gave birth to a new baby boy. They named him Benjamin after Josiah's brother.

Josiah bundled the new baby into blankets and carried him across the street to South Church. Puritan parents viewed life as a mighty struggle between God and the devil, and since death might snatch their infants at any moment, it was best to quickly baptize a newborn. If death came, the child's cleansed soul was ready for heaven.

But Ben did not die—he thrived, healthy and strong, in a home filled with brothers and sisters. Two more baby girls joined the Franklin mob. The last one, named Jane, became young Ben's favorite of all his siblings.

GROWING UP
IN BOSTON

❧ Roughly 7,000 people called the thriving town of Boston home. As the third-largest shipping center in the whole British Empire, Boston's waterfront rocked with ships and swarming seamen loading and unloading cargo along the wharves. Josiah prospered enough to move his family from the tiny house, once crammed elbow-to-elbow with 14 children, to a larger home and shop in the center of town. By the time Ben was six, many of his elder siblings had left to make their own way in the world.

Rivers, bays, and inlets led to the sea, and young Ben Franklin played often "in and about" the water. He learned to swim

Who Were the Puritans?

JOSIAH FRANKLIN belonged to the Puritan church. In the 1500s some members of the official Church of England felt their church followed too many Catholic rituals. Their church needed "purifying."

Puritans believed every person could (and should) read, study, and discuss the Bible. They believed in sermons to enlighten the soul. They believed each church congregation should be self-governing, not run by bishops or a pope. They held strict views on moral conduct. Puritans believed men showed respect for God by working hard. A man's success showed that God smiled upon him. Boston, founded in 1630 as the Puritan's shining "City on a Hill," became the center for Puritan America.

Puritans loved words like *diligence*, *obedience*, *duty*, and *industry*—meaning hard work. Idleness and time wasting opened the door to temptations from the "great deluder," Satan. In 1715, Isaac Watts wrote a poem to turn children from idleness and mischief.

How doth the little busy Bee
Improve each shining Hour,
And gather Honey all the day
From every opening Flower!...
In Works of Labour or of Skill
I would be busy too:
For Satan finds some Mischief still
For idle Hands to do.

❧ GROW CRYSTAL CANDY ❧

Rock candy is made from growing sugar crystals. This candy has been around for centuries. It was also used as a medicine to soothe sore throats.

MATERIALS

Adult supervision required

- 1 pint-size canning jar, washed clean and dried
- 1 clean nail
- Hammer
- 1 quart pan
- ¾ cup of water
- 2 rounded cups of sugar (a bit more than two cups)
- Food coloring (optional)
- Tape (optional)
- Wooden skewers, about 10 inches long (in packages at the grocery store)
- Utility knife
- Small frying pan
- Spoon
- 2 tablespoons of sugar
- 1 teaspoon of water
- Butter knife
- Plate

First, use a hammer to punch two nail holes in the canning jar lid about 1½ inches apart.

STEP 1: Make Rock Candy Syrup

In a quart pan, bring ¾ cup of water to a boil over medium heat. Stir the sugar into the boiling water. Keep stirring for about two minutes until the liquid turns clear. Cook for one more minute to make sure all the sugar crystals have dissolved, but do not overcook!

Carefully pour the hot syrup into the canning jar. Add a few drops of food coloring if you'd like. Let the syrup cool to room temperature. This may take a while.

STEP 2: Seed the Skewers

While the rock candy syrup cools, you can "seed" the skewers. You must seed the wooden skewer so that the sugar crystals have something to attach to. Have an adult cut a 10-inch skewer in half with a utility knife. Each piece should be about 5 inches long.

To a frying pan, add 2 tablespoons of sugar and 1 teaspoon of water. Cook over medium heat, stirring constantly. The mixture will eventually turn into a thick liquid syrup. But do not let the syrup get too hot or it will turn dark.

Turn off the heat. Use a butter knife to quickly spread the skewers, one at a time, with the syrup. Before the syrup hardens, hold each skewer over a plate and sprinkle it with sugar.

Soak the frying pan before cleaning.

STEP 3: Make Rock Candy

Stick the two unsugared ends of the seeded skewers through the holes in the jar lid. If they

do not stay in without sliding, lightly tape them in place from the top.

Lower the sticks into the cooled syrup. Adjust the sticks so they do not touch.

Place the jar in a warm spot, between 70 and 80 degrees Fahrenheit, for **one week**. Near a TV is usually a good place. Every day watch the crystals as they grow on the skewers.

After one week lift the lid holding the skewer sticks and pour off the syrup. If necessary, break the rock candy away from the bottom of the jar.

Let the candy dry on a clean plate. Once dry, eat and enjoy— or use it to stir hot tea for a sweet drink.

1751 ❈ His book, *Experiments and Observations on Electricity*, is published in London

Founds the Pennsylvania Academy, later known as the University of Pennsylvania

1752 ❈ Famous kite experiment proves lightning is electricity

1757–62 ❈ In London as agent for the colony of Pennsylvania

1762 ❈ Returns to Philadelphia

1764 ❈ Back in London

1774 ❈ The Hutchinson Letters Affair damages Franklin's reputation

1775 ❈ Back in Philadelphia; serves in Second Continental Congress

1776 ❈ Signs the Declaration of Independence

Serves as president of Pennsylvania Constitutional Convention

Becomes American commissioner to France

1778 ❈ Negotiates Treaty of Alliance with France

Appointed sole minister plenipotentiary to France

1782 ❈ Helps negotiate Treaty of Peace with Great Britain; final treaty signed September 1783

1783 ❈ Witnesses the first hot-air balloon flights in Paris

1785 ❈ Returns to Philadelphia

1787 ❈ Elected president of the Pennsylvania Society for Promoting the Abolition of Slavery and the Relief of Negroes Unlawfully Held in Bondage

Serves as a delegate to the Constitutional Convention

1790 ❈ Dies on April 17 at age 84

NOTE TO READERS

MANY OF Benjamin Franklin's writings have survived over 200 years. When you read Franklin's original words, you'll notice that spelling, grammar, and punctuation have often changed over the centuries. Also, sometimes words were capitalized in the middle of a sentence—this was common and proper in writings from the 1700s.

Preface

THE RUNAWAY

⟡ ONE DAY, he'd be a famous man in Philadelphia, in America, and across the sea in Europe. But on a Sunday morning in early October 1723, the 17-year-old was simply running away from his home in Boston. He climbed out of a boat onto Philadelphia's Market Street Wharf, exhausted, his stomach growling with hunger, his plain working clothes grimy from the trip. The few coins in his pocket weighed almost nothing. He knew not a soul in Philadelphia. Where should he even look for a place to sleep that night?

He wandered up Market Street, gazing all about him. At a bakery he handed over a precious coin for three puffy, golden rolls. With the extra rolls stuffed one under each arm, he munched his way up the street. His coat pockets bulged with some additional shirts and stockings stuffed inside. He noted a girl standing in a doorway who seemed to think his appearance perfectly ridiculous.

He wandered down Chestnut Street and turned onto Walnut, all the while stuffing down his bread. But his wandering only brought him in a great circle back to the river. There, he handed his extra rolls to a mother and child he'd met on the boat.

A flock of people headed up Market Street, and he joined them, shuffling into the hushed Quaker Meeting House. Sitting down, the lad looked around the plain building. No minister rose to speak, as in

the Sunday church services in Boston. In the silence, he promptly fell asleep.

How do you start a new life in a new place with nothing to call your own? The runaway teenager possessed a brightly sharp and curious brain. He worked hard, planned hard, and saved hard. His natural charm and ease with people, from common folk to great gentlemen, sped his climb of success in colonial America. The lad's name was Benjamin Franklin, and on this October morning he started from scratch to earn his place in the world.

Benjamin Franklin

AMERICAN GENIUS

❧ I ❧

"AS A YOUNG GENIUS"

I N OCTOBER 1683, Josiah Franklin, his wife Anne, and their three small children gazed hungrily for their first sight of land. They'd left England nine long weeks before on a cramped ship packed tight with 100 other passengers and crew. Twenty-five-year-old Josiah hoped not only to find religious freedom in New England but also to better support his growing family. In Massachusetts a man could live more cheaply and earn more for his hard work. In Boston the Franklins would build a new life.

Josiah labored as a silk and fabric dyer in England. But the Puritans of Boston fined people for wearing fancy clothes or for dressing above their place in society.

To make a go of things in the New World, Josiah tackled a new trade—he became a tallow chandler, a maker of candles and soap.

On the corner of Milk Street and High Street, Josiah and Anne rented a two-and-a-half-story clapboard house that also served as Josiah's shop. The ground floor had one long room. To protect the main house from fire, the kitchen was out back in a separate building. Across the street stood South Church, the newest of Boston's three church congregations.

More children filled the Franklin house, but like many homes in colonial America, death stalked the family, too. A baby son died. Then Anne Franklin died, leaving behind a week-old son, who soon followed his mother to the grave. Left with five children to care for, a trade to work, and a shop and home to run, Josiah needed a new wife and helpmate. People remarried quickly in colonial America. Five months after Anne's death, Josiah married Abiah Folger. Her father, Peter Folger, had been an early settler of New England.

Over the next 12 years, Abiah and Josiah's family grew, though tragedy always waited on the doorstep. Two more little sons died,

Benjamin Franklin's birthplace on Milk Street in Boston.

and handle a boat. He fashioned flippers for his hands and feet to see if they helped him swim faster. And once, he used a kite to pull himself back and forth across a pond.

Ben's friends looked to him as their captain, even though sometimes he led them "into Scrapes." Once, after they'd trampled their favorite fishing spot into a muddy mess, Ben proposed building a proper wharf to fish from. One night he and his pals lugged away a heap of stones meant for a new house. The boys constructed their stone wharf, but the next morning all was discovered—the missing stones, the newly built wharf, and the boys' identities! "Several of us were corrected by our Fathers," remembered Franklin, "and tho' I pleaded the Usefulness of the Work, mine convinc'd me that nothing was useful which was not honest." In colonial America, *corrections* usually meant a spanking or whipping.

Young Ben reads by candlelight.

The Expensive Whistle

ONE DAY Ben came upon a boy blowing a whistle. Oh, how Ben wanted that whistle! He offered the boy all the coins in his pocket and arrived home to show off his new treasure. But his brothers and sister scoffed that Ben had paid much more than the whistle was worth. Ben cried with frustration over wasting his money. The whistle now gave him little pleasure. Franklin learned from the whistle and the taunts of his siblings. One of the things he became most famous for was being careful and frugal with his money.

SHOOT A GAME OF MARBLES

Marbles was a popular game for children in colonial America. Most marbles at the time were made of fired clay, not glass.

MATERIALS

* Masking tape or blue painter tape (for playing indoors)
* Chalk or a stick (for playing outside)
* Marbles, including several larger ones

On a bare floor, indoors, make a circle about 15 inches across using pieces of masking tape. Or, if you are playing outside, you can use chalk to draw a circle or scratch out a circle in the dirt using a stick.

Each player keeps a "shooter" marble. This is usually a larger marble. Put the rest of the marbles in the center of the circle.

Draw a line about a foot away from the circle. This is the *taw line*. Each player kneels behind the line and shoots his or her marble into the circle. To shoot, face your palm up, hold the marble in your curled forefinger, and flick it with your thumb. Or, you can set your marble on the ground and flick it with your forefinger.

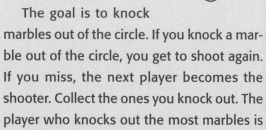

The goal is to knock marbles out of the circle. If you knock a marble out of the circle, you get to shoot again. If you miss, the next player becomes the shooter. Collect the ones you knock out. The player who knocks out the most marbles is the winner.

But young Ben did not always stir up trouble. The lad also possessed a passion for books and learning. Franklin later recalled, "I do not remember when I could not read." He read anything and everything he could lay his hands on. Josiah wondered if he had a scholar on his hands. Should he train Ben to serve as a minister, one of the most highly regarded and respected professions?

Josiah enrolled eight-year-old Ben in the Boston Latin School, the fast track for boys heading to the minister training ground of Harvard. Ben excelled, swiftly climbing to the head of the class. But Josiah pulled Ben from the school after less than a year, perhaps fearing the expense of a Harvard education. Or maybe he had a feeling Ben would not make a very good minister. The bright and curious boy sometimes offered opinions a bit strong for his family. One fall, as the Franklins salted and prepared their meat to store for the winter, Ben suggested they bless all the meat at once to save time saying grace before each meal. Perhaps not minister material!

Josiah instead sent Ben to a school that concentrated on reading, writing, and math, a subject Ben failed and "made no Progress in it." After a year Ben Franklin's formal school days ended, but he'd spent more time in school than most children in colonial America.

LEARNING A TRADE

Most colonial boys' education centered on an apprenticeship. Parents signed papers binding their child in service to a craftsman or tradesman. In exchange for the child's work, the master taught him the skills needed for a future job. An apprentice belonged to his master and enjoyed few freedoms. The apprentice could not leave the master's home or business without permission. Older apprentices were forbidden to marry, gamble, or go out to taverns.

At age ten, Ben joined his father in the tallow shop. Tallow, the fat from cattle, was simmered for hours with lye, made from wood ash, to make soap and candles. Ben recalled his jobs "cutting Wick for the Candles, filling the Dipping Mold, & the Molds for cast Candles, attending the Shop, going of Errands" and soon hated the smelly, hot, tedious work.

Josiah feared unhappy Ben might run away and become a sailor, and he'd already had one son perish at sea. He explored other options with his son. He walked Ben about Boston, observing the many craftsmen and tradesmen at work—silversmiths, tanners, coopers (barrel makers), bricklayers, joiners (furniture makers), blacksmiths, and more. In the end Josiah apprenticed Ben in 1718

❧ POUR A BAR OF SOAP ❧

In Josiah Franklin's chandler shop, soap was made from boiling together a smelly mixture of lye and animal fat, not something we'd really like to use to clean ourselves today.

MATERIALS
Adult supervision required
- Butter knife
- Clear glycerin from a craft store (it might come in 1½-inch cubes or a larger block)
- Glass measuring cup
- Spoon
- Microwave oven
- Soap coloring and fragrance (optional)
- Decorative plastic soap molds from a craft store

Using a butter knife, cut off two to four squares of glycerin, depending on the size of the soap mold. Two or three squares make about one small bar of soap.

Put the squares into a glass measuring cup. Put the cup in a microwave oven and melt on high for 40 seconds. If the glycerin is not all melted, add 10 more seconds.

If you wish, add a few drops of coloring into the melted glycerin and stir with the spoon. If you want a deeper color, add more drops. If you are using fragrance, add a drop to the melted soap.

Pour the glycerin from the measuring cup into the soap mold. Let the soap cool and firm up, about 30 minutes. When it has reached room temperature, tip the mold over and use gentle pressure to pop out the bar of soap. If it sticks, run hot water over the bottom of the mold and try again.

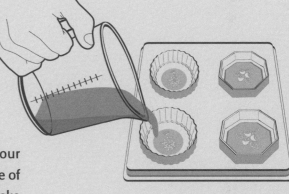

If your soap mold has places for several bars of soap, try melting and pouring one bar at a time to make each soap a different color. Just rinse out the measuring cup before melting the next batch. Let them all cool at the same time.

DIP CANDLES

Ben worked in his father's soap-making and candle-making shop and hated the hot, smelly work. Colonial candles were usually made of animal fat boiled with lye, poured into molds or from wicks dipped into the melted tallow.

MATERIALS

Adult supervision required

- Sharp knife
- Candle wax (from a craft store)
- Old can or pot for melting wax, and another larger pot to make a double boiler (you can buy pots at a craft store, too)
- Candle coloring or scent (optional)
- 24–28 inches cotton candle wick
- Wooden spoon

With an adult helping, cut or shave hunks of wax and put them into your melting pot or old can. Set the melting pot inside another larger pot. Add water to the bottom pot. Over medium heat, start melting the wax. This could take a while, but keep an eye on it.

When the wax is melted, add coloring and scent, if desired. Turn off the stove.

You can make two candles. Cut your wicks 12 to 14 inches long. Tie one end of the wick to a wooden spoon handle. Quickly dip the wicks, one at a time, into the melted wax. Lift the wick. Do not let the wick stay in the hot wax too long when you are dipping or you'll melt the wax you've already put on the wick.

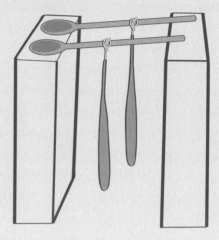

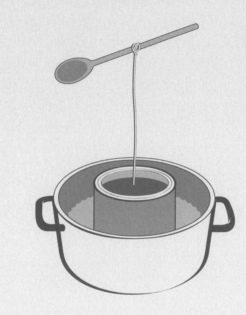

For the first few dips, gently pull both ends of the wick to keep the wax forming on a straight line, so the finished candle will not be crooked. Keep dipping the wick into the wax. Each time the wax builds up a bit more. It takes *many* dips to make a candle. Let the wax set up and cool for a few minutes between dips. You can rest the wooded spoon between two canisters, cereal boxes, or the like to cool.

When your candles are the desired thickness, cut each bottom off straight with a knife. Cut each wick to a half inch long. Now you can use your candles.

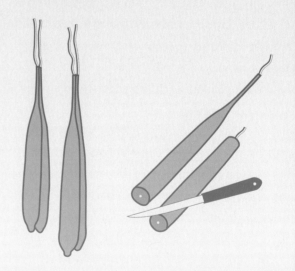

to one of his elder sons, Ben's half-brother James, who was a printer. James had Ben, now twelve years old, sign an unusually long apprenticeship of nine years.

The two brothers probably did not know each other very well. Older by nine years, James had studied printing in England before returning to Boston and setting up his own shop. Ben, along with James and his other apprentices, boarded with another family. Already keen on living a frugal life, Ben made a deal with James: he'd feed himself if James would hand over half the money he paid for Ben's food. James agreed. Ben squirreled away some of the money by eating a meager diet of water, bread, raisins, and sometimes a biscuit or tart.

As much as Ben disliked working for James, who sometimes beat him, printing suited young Ben much better than the candle and soap business. He loved being around the printed pages full of information,

(LEFT) Ben pours tallow into candle molds.
(RIGHT) Ben prepares to ink the type by rolling the ink between two padded leather "balls."

loved hearing the news customers bantered about the shop. The place smelled of ink and leather and wood and paper. Crowded cases holding compartments of tiny metal letters lined the walls. The capital letters were stored in the upper cases.

The shop printed the *Boston Gazette* for the newspaper owner and did all types of print work: pamphlets, advertisements, stationery, government laws—whatever a customer needed. Ben learned to set the letters in trays, letter by letter, word by word, line by line, row by row. He dabbed and rolled the trays with ink and set them on the heavy printing press. The press forced the paper against the inked letters. As Ben grew tall and strong, he easily shouldered his share of the hard physical work lifting heavy trays of metal letters, carrying reams of paper, and handling the printing press.

JOY IN READING

❧ BEN FOUND real joy in reading and writing—skills that could turn a lowly apprentice into a gifted printer. Printers often wrote their own articles or pamphlets and edited the work of others. Ben pored over the books in James's small library. Few people in colonial America owned scarce and precious books. Ben discovered a way to get his hands on even more books. He befriended the apprentices of Boston's booksellers. His friends let Ben sneak books from the shops, read them overnight, and return the volumes in the morning.

Ben carved out time for reading and studying. At night, early in the morning, or on Sundays, when by law he should have been in church, Ben hid himself away with his books. Among his favorites were John Bunyan's *Pilgrim's Progress*, John Locke's *An Essay Concerning Human Understanding*, Roman historian Plutarch's *Lives*, Daniel Defoe's *Essay on Projects*, and Cotton Mather's *Bonifacius: Essays to Do Good*. Ben knew Mather, a Boston minister and leading member of society.

The books gave young Ben "a Turn of Thinking." He tried new ideas. For a time he became a vegetarian, mastering the boiling of potatoes, rice, and hasty pudding. He experimented with religious ideas such as Deism—a belief that a Superior Being created the world and then left human beings alone. He dropped his habit of arguing and contradicting people and instead adopted a new policy. Following the ideas of the ancient Greek philosopher Socrates, Franklin began asking people seemingly innocent questions that slowly led them to see his side of the argument! He delighted in becoming "the humble Enquirer and Doubter." He found this method "safest to myself & very embarrassing to those against whom I used it."

Ben especially devoured Joseph Addison's and Richard Steele's essays in the *Spectator*, a British publication. Addison and Steele pricked society's weaknesses through humor and wit, not by lecturing with sermons. "I thought the Writing excellent," Ben wrote, "& wished if possible to imitate it." He read the essays over and over. He copied them out and recopied them. He scribbled notes. He mixed up the essays' sections, then put them back together to see how Addison and Steele organized their writings. In this painstaking manner, Ben mastered "the Arrangement of Thoughts," the skill of engaging readers and winning them over with a clear argument.

THE *NEW ENGLAND COURANT*

❧ Only a few men published newspapers in Boston. The papers bore the label "published by authority," meaning the Puritan government granted permission to print. These papers played it safe, steering clear of controversy or tweaking the noses of Boston's Puritan leaders. They mostly reprinted

months-old European news and official proclamations.

In August 1721, James Franklin began publishing his own newspaper, the *New England Courant*. James's paper was not "published by authority," and James did not play it safe.

❧ HASTY PUDDING ❧

*H*asty pudding was one of many popular ground-corn recipes in the American colonies. It was a dish that the teenage Ben learned to make for his vegetarian diet. He also ate this affordable food to save money.

MATERIALS
Adult Supervision Required
- Mixing bowl
- Measuring cup
- 1 cup cornmeal
- 1 cup cold water
- Saucepan
- 3 cups water
- ½ teaspoon salt
- Spoon or wire whisk
- Butter
- Maple syrup, brown sugar, molasses, or cream (your choice)

In a bowl combine 1 cup of cornmeal and 1 cup of cold water.

In a heavy saucepan bring 3 cups of water and ½ teaspoon of salt to a boil. Then, carefully whisk in the cornmeal mixture. Turn down the burner. Cook the mixture for 10 to 15 minutes over low heat, stirring once in a while.

Spoon the hasty pudding into bowls. Top with a pat of butter and your choice of maple syrup, brown sugar, molasses, or cream.

This recipe makes six to seven servings.

The two- to four-page paper appeared each week, printing biting satires poking fun at many of Boston's elite men and the Puritan church. Soon an establishment paper, the *Boston Gazette and News Letter,* denounced James's efforts as a "Notorious, Scandalous Paper" full of "Nonsense, Unmannerliness… Immorality, Arrogancy… Lyes… all tending to Quarrels and Divisions" meant to corrupt the "Minds and Manners of New England."

On Boston's streets Ben hawked his brother's scandalous paper, as well as some ballads he'd written himself! He shared James's view that the Puritan government needed a bit of criticism. The *Courant* circulated around Boston—shared, passed along, and read not only by society's upper crust but by "middling sorts" and the city's artisans, as well.

But even while agreeing with James's jabs at authority, Ben chafed at his brother's authority over *him.* The apprenticeship proved difficult for Ben. Eventually he looked for any chance to shorten or break his bond.

"THE SPECKLED MONSTER"

🐎 In April 1721 the most feared disease in colonial America—smallpox—arrived in Boston on a ship carrying "the speckled monster" among its crew and passengers. Many believed an angry God had sent the disease as punishment to kill and scar. Using his new paper and the smallpox crisis, James Franklin launched attacks on a leading Puritan physician and minister, Cotton Mather, and his supporters.

Cotton Mather had lost 2 wives and 13 of his 15 children to measles or smallpox outbreaks. Mather learned from one of his Afri-

Ben sells his ballads on the streets of Boston.

can slaves that he could prevent smallpox through a process called inoculation: a physician scratched a small amount of smallpox pus into the skin of a healthy person. Those inoculated usually caught only a mild case of smallpox. Their body's defenses, once tested by smallpox, fought off the disease and made them safe from future outbreaks. Mather urgently promoted inoculation to save hundreds of Boston's citizens.

But others viewed inoculation with suspicion—it did not make sense that you saved someone by giving him or her a dose of the

Cotton Mather

disease. Why should Christian men trust the word of a slave, "the Way of the Heathen"? And if God sent smallpox to punish Boston, then life or death was up to God, not men—even church leaders like Mather. Did men have the right to step in to help people? Did God send cures as well as sending the disease?

The smallpox controversy offered the *Courant* a rousing start. The war of words in Boston's newspapers kept Ben busy setting type and running the press. Words spiraled into violence when someone threw a bomb of gunpowder and turpentine—which failed to explode—into Mather's house. It carried a note: "Cotton Mather, You dog. Dam you: I'll inoculate you with this, with a Pox to you."

In the end, however, Mather was proved correct. Half of Boston's people caught smallpox, and 842 died. Of the 242 people inoculated, only 6 died. James's war with Mather and others put him on a collision course with the Puritan authorities.

SILENCE DOGOOD SOUNDS OFF

ON MARCH 26, 1722, the first of 16 letters appeared in the *Courant* penned by a respectable, middle-aged widow named

Silence Dogood. In reality, 16-year-old Ben Franklin created her out of his imagination, wrote the letters, and slipped them under the *Courant*'s door at night. In the first letter, the widow Dogood introduced herself to her readers. Born on a ship, she recalled her father standing on the deck "rejoycing at my Birth" when "a merciless wave entered the Ship, and in one Moment carry'd him beyond Reprieve. Thus was the *first* Day which I saw, the last that was seen by my Father." At the print shop, Ben listened with amusement as everyone wondered who this tart-tongued "Silence Dogood" was.

Through Silence Dogood, Ben poked fun at Boston's elite, including the students of Harvard, a place he had once hoped to attend. Dogood labeled Harvard's students "Dunces and Blockheads" who had been admitted to the college because of their fat wallets. In return for their money, the students learned "how to carry themselves handsomely, and enter a room genteely," and when their days at Harvard ended, they left school "as great Blockheads as ever, only more proud and self-conceited."

In another letter the widow Dogood describes herself—a pretty good description of Benjamin Franklin, as well.

Ben Franklin works the printing press. Notice the type cases on the back left wall and the apprentices' leather aprons.

Know then, That I am an Enemy to Vice, and a Friend to Vertue. I am ... a great Forgiver of Private Injuries: A Hearty Lover of the Clergy and all good Men, and a Mortal Enemy to arbitrary Government and unlimited Power. I am naturally very Jealous for the Rights and Liberties of my Country; and the least appearance of an Incroachment on those invaluable Priviledges is apt to make my Blood boil exceedingly.... To be brief; I am courteous and affable, good humour'd (unless I am provok'd), handsome, and sometimes witty, but always Sir, Your Friend and Humble Servant, Silence Dogood.

Eventually James discovered Silence Dogood's identity. Ben's trick riled James. He felt that Ben's success swelled his head with vanity and encouraged disobedience. Ben recalled, "I thought he demean'd me too much in some he requir'd of me, who from a Brother expected more Indulgence," Later, Benjamin Franklin admitted he was "too saucy and provoking" of his brother. But at the time, confident and rebellious Ben thought only about escaping.

TIME TO LEAVE

JAMES'S BATTLES for a free press eventually landed him in jail. On June 11, 1722, he'd published an article accusing government officials of being in league with pirates smuggling along the coast. The court ordered the brothers hauled in to face a judge. The court let Ben off with a warning but imprisoned James. Ben wrote,

During my Brother's confinement, which I resented a good deal, notwithstanding our private Differences, I had the Management of the Paper, and I made bold to give our Rulers some Rubs in it, which my Brother took very kindly, while others began to consider me in an unfavorable Light, as a young Genius that had a Turn for Libeling and Satyr [satire].

James spent three weeks in jail. But that did not keep him out of further troubles. In February 1723 the government officially denied James the right to publish the *New England Courant*. James wormed his way around this by publishing the paper under Ben's name. To do this, he and Ben signed a new and secret apprentice agreement.

But Ben knew James could never enforce the new agreement. Ben finally had the break he'd been waiting for. "I had already made myself a little obnoxious to the governing party," he recalled, "and it was likely I might if I stay'd soon bring myself into Scrapes, [for] my indiscrete Disputations [arguments] about Religion began to make me pointed at with Horror by good People."

But most of all, he could no longer stand working for James. In late September 1723, Ben sold a few books to raise cash, and without a word to even his parents, he broke his binding apprenticeship and ran away.

2

"A YOUNG MAN OF PROMISING PARTS"

A FRIEND ARRANGED Ben's passage on a boat out of Boston, and three days and 300 miles later he arrived in New York. He offered his services at a print shop owned by William Bradford. The man had no job for Ben, but his son living in Philadelphia might need a lad in his printing business. Ben determined to try his luck there. He endured drenching rains on shipboard, walked 50 miles, picked up another boat, and then when no winds filled

the sails, helped row all the way to Philadelphia. He arrived miserable, hungry, poor, and exhausted to wander the city's streets before falling asleep in a Quaker meetinghouse.

Ben found room and board at the Crooked Billet and crashed, spending most of his first two days in Philadelphia sleeping. Then, tidying up as best he could, Ben presented himself at Andrew Bradford's printing shop. Like his father in New York, the younger Bradford had no employment for the run-

away. He fed Ben breakfast and sent him to the only other printing shop in Philadelphia, which was owned by Samuel Keimer.

Franklin hurried to Keimer's print shop and found him working with an "old shatter'd Press, and one small worn-out Fount of English"—not very promising to his eyes. Keimer tested Ben's skills and eventually hired him. The teenager soon realized he knew more about printing than either Bradford or Keimer.

(BELOW) Ben arrives in Philadelphia and walks past Deborah Read, his future wife. (RIGHT) Philadelphia

IN 1681, King Charles II paid off a debt by granting William Penn vast lands in America to found a new colony. As the owner, or proprietor, of Pennsylvania (founded in 1682), Penn held great power—he could set up the colony any way he liked, decide how the legislature would run, name a governor, select the governor's council, and pick judges. The king granted these powers in return for Penn shouldering the risk and expense of settling British subjects in America. A proprietor, however, could reap huge rewards by selling lands and collecting fees.

Penn, a member of the Society of Friends, also known as Quakers, hoped to create a haven for persecuted Quakers in his new colony. Unlike Puritan Massachusetts, Penn's colony was recognized for its tolerance toward religion.

Penn established Philadelphia—Greek for "city of brotherly love"—where the Schuylkill River flowed into the Delaware River. Ships sailed up the Delaware River from the Atlantic Ocean to load and unload tons of cargo at Philadelphia. When Ben Franklin arrived in the 1720s, the city boasted a population of about 7,000 citizens.

Immigrants flocked to Penn's colony, not only English but Scots, Irish, and Germans, too. Many spent their first seven years or more in America as indentured servants, bound to their masters for the payment of their ship's passage. By the mid-1700s, over 23,000 people called Philadelphia home, making it the largest city in the 13 colonies. Philadelphia attracted scientists, artists, and craftsmen, a perfect backdrop for Ben Franklin's talents. But Pennsylvania remained a proprietary colony. William Penn's children inherited the ownership of Pennsylvania, and later Benjamin Franklin would clash with Penn's powerful sons.

William Penn lands in "Pennsylvania."

Ben lodged at the home of John Read; he especially liked his landlord's daughter, Deborah. Never shy, Ben sought other working-class young men who shared his passion for reading and conversation. He regaled listeners with his storytelling and took pains to get along with people. He attracted people not only through his wit and good sense but also just by walking into a room. At about six feet tall—taller than the average man—and with a well-muscled body toned from years of swimming and the heavy work in a printing shop, Ben radiated strength.

GOVERNOR KEITH TAKES NOTICE

❧ BEN FRANKLIN described his full life in Philadelphia in a letter to one of his brothers-in-law, a shipmaster and trader named Robert Holmes. Captain Holmes "happened to be in company" with Pennsylvania governor Sir William Keith when Ben's letter arrived. Amazed that a 17-year-old wrote with such style and flare, the governor deemed Ben a "young Man of promising Parts, and therefore should be encouraged." In the 1700s a young man of low birth needed a sponsor or patron to get ahead. When the governor showed up at the print shop and invited Ben to dinner, "I

was not a little surpriz'd," recalled Ben, "and Keimer star'd like a Pig poison'd."

Fed up with the only two printers in Philadelphia, Keith encouraged Ben to open his own print shop. He pushed the teenager to return to Boston and seek financial help from his father for the venture. His head swelled with visions of his bright future, Ben sailed to Boston and surprised his family in April 1724. Everyone welcomed the runaway home… everyone except James. Cocky Ben visited his brother's shop, showing off a new suit, displaying a new watch, and flashing around gifts of money to James's workers. James turned on his heel and ignored Ben, insulted by his runaway apprentice's behavior.

Ben also visited Cotton Mather, a man whose writings he admired. The smallpox press war laid aside, Mather welcomed the younger Franklin into his library. The two continued talking while they walked down a narrow passage with a low beam running across it. Suddenly Mather cried, "Stoop, Stoop!" Ben didn't understand until he conked his head against the beam. "He was a man," wrote Franklin, "that never missed any occasion of giving instruction, and upon this he said to me: 'You are young, and have the world before you; STOOP as you go through it, and you will miss many hard thumps.'"

Josiah, though pleased his son had captured the attention of Pennsylvania's governor, turned down Ben's request for money. Josiah even questioned Keith's judgment in wanting to set up an inexperienced teenager in business. If Ben still desired to open his own shop in a few years, and he'd worked and saved toward his goal, then Josiah might help. Until then, his son needed to learn respect, stop poking fun at others, and grow up.

Ben stopped in New York City on the way back to Philadelphia. The governor of the colony, William Burnet, heard about the lad traveling with a trunk of books and invited him over for a chat. Apparently a well-read, clever young man made a rare and interesting character. Ben recalled, "The Govr. treated me with great civility, show'd me his library, which was a very large one, & we had a good deal of conversation about Books & Authors. This was the second Governor who had done me the Honour to take Notice of me, which to a poor Boy like me was very pleasing."

With no money from Josiah, Governor Keith declared he'd help establish Ben's printing business. He urged him to sail for London and buy what he needed. The governor promised to supply letters of introduction and a line of credit for Ben to purchase equipment and paper.

Governor Keith approaches Ben Franklin in Keimer's print shop.

"If You Eat One Another"

ON THE voyage back from Boston, calm winds held the boat off Cape Cod. Some passengers decided to fish for their supper. As a vegetarian, Ben had not eaten meat for a while, and the smell of fish frying in the pan made his mouth water. Then he remembered that, "when the Fish were opened, I saw smaller Fish taken out of their Stomachs:—Then, thought I, if you eat one another, I don't see why we mayn't eat you. So I din'd upon Cod very heartily... returning only now & then occasionally to a vegetable Diet." Wasn't it lucky, he thought, "to be a *reasonable Creature*, since it enables one to find or make a Reason for every thing one has a mind to do."

While Ben waited for the big trip, he continued working at Keimer's and courted Deborah Read. Franklin felt a "great Respect & Affection for her." Deborah's father had died, and her mother suggested they wait until Ben returned from England and set up his shop before jumping into marriage. "Perhaps," Franklin later remembered, "she thought my Expectations not so well founded as I imagined them to be." When Ben sailed, he and Deborah had "Interchang'd Promises" to marry.

In November 1724, Ben sailed for England with his friend James Ralph. He carried high hopes with him, including the hope that letters from Governor Keith lurked in the stuffed mailbags headed to London. Ben spent the voyage meeting new people, including a Quaker merchant named Thomas Denham. Denham quietly warned him not to rely too much on Governor Keith, for "no one who knew him had the smallest Dependence on him, and he laughed at the Notion of the Governor's giving me a letter of Credit, having as he said no Credit to give."

Unfortunately for Ben, this proved true. The mailbag held no letters. "He wished to please every body," he wrote of Keith, "and having little to give, he gave expectations." But a young man could not live on expectations. Ben needed a job.

A LAD IN LONDON

🐦 LONDON DWARFED both Boston and Philadelphia with a population of over half a million people. Many were like Ben, new arrivals crowding into the old city's narrow lanes and busy streets. London bustled with merchants and shopkeepers, traders, artisans, and craftsmen. Below these comfortable skilled workers on the social ladder clung a mass of poor people: beggars, sailors, street vendors, servants, and laborers. At the very tip of society the king and his aristocrats lived in luxury and richness unimaginable in the colonies. They spent more on a single banquet than an American might earn in a lifetime.

Ben quickly found work at a famous London printing house. He and James Ralph lodged together and freely spent their money attending plays and other amusements. Ben loved hanging out at coffee shops, listening to the conversations. He scribbled letters introducing himself and seeking introductions to famous and interesting people. One man promised to introduce him to the famous scientist Sir Isaac Newton—but the meeting never took place.

James Ralph admitted he never meant to return home to his wife and child in the colonies. Ben too caught the wave of unfaithfulness and forgot his engagement to

Deborah, "to whom I never wrote more than one letter, & that was to let her know I was not likely soon to return." He hung out with "low women."

As money flew from his pockets in amusements and loans to Ralph, Ben realized he'd better shape up. He began work at one of the best printing houses in London, moved to cheaper lodgings, and slashed his rations. For breakfast he dug into hot-water gruel spiced with pepper, breadcrumbs, and a bit of butter. He downed half an anchovy, bread and butter, and a half-pint of ale for supper. He worked hard and impressed his employer and fellow workers, who called him the "Water American" because he refused to spend all his hard-earned wages on ale.

One young man hired Ben to teach him how to swim. Other gentlemen expressed curiosity, for few people, even sailors, could swim. One day, remembered Franklin, "I stript & leapt into the River, & swam from near Chelsea to Blackfryars, performing on the Way many Feats of Activity both upon & under Water, that surpriz'd and pleas'd those to whom they were Novelties." He even considered traveling Europe to teach swimming and perform demonstrations.

But one day Ben met his friend from the ship, Mr. Denham, who encouraged Ben to return to Philadelphia and work for him as a shop clerk. After 18 months in London, the thought of home seemed sweet. He agreed to Denham's offer of assistance, and on July 23, 1726, Ben Franklin left England for Philadelphia.

The printing press Ben Franklin trained on in London.

A RATIONAL CREATURE

ON THE 11-week voyage home, Ben kept a journal, noting his observations of rainbows, dolphins, seaweed, crabs—all things of air and sea. More importantly, the 20-year-old mulled over his life and determined he needed a "Plan For Future Conduct." "Let me therefore make some resolutions," he wrote, "and form some scheme of action, that henceforth I may live in all respects like a rational creature."

Ben penned a few basic rules. He would be "extremely frugal … till I have paid what I owe." He would not lose focus "by any foolish project of suddenly growing rich." Hard work and patience would carry him through to a comfortable life. He vowed "to speak truth in every instance; to give nobody expectations that are not likely to be answered." He promised to "speak ill of no man whatever."

Denham died shortly after the return to Philadelphia, and Ben returned to Keimer's printing house. There he managed and trained the other workers. He became the first person in America to make type from a mold. When Keimer received a job printing money for the colony of New Jersey, Ben designed and engraved the copperplates so ornately that the money could not easily be counterfeited.

The contrast between untidy, grouchy Keimer and young, energetic Franklin, radiating charm and skill, struck print shop customers. People invited Ben to their homes and introduced him to their friends. His web of friends spread and became of "great Use to me, as I occasionally was to some of them."

B. FRANKLIN, PRINTER

FRANKLIN FINALLY had enough of making Keimer look good. In 1728, he and another Keimer employee, Hugh Meredith, opened their own printing business. Meredith's father supplied the money. They rented a house for their shop, and to help pay rent they leased space to a glazier (glass worker). The glazier's wife provided Ben's meals.

Within hours after opening they had their first customer. Ben worked backbreaking long hours, sometimes till 11:00 at night or later, to build his business. "And this industry," he wrote, "visible to our Neighbours began to give us Character and Credit."

Ben worked to woo a few top printing jobs away from Andrew Bradford. When Bradford printed an address from the governor to the Pennsylvania legislature, Franklin thought the work coarse and blundering. He reprinted the address "elegantly & correctly" and sent a copy to every House member. The next year the House voted to give his print shop their government business.

Ben supported the idea that Pennsylvania needed more paper money in circulation to boost the economy. He wrote a pamphlet titled *A Modest Enquiry into the Nature & Necessity of a Paper Currency.* Who soon won the job for printing the new money? Ben called the profitable work "a great Help to me.—This was another Advantage gain'd by my being able to write."

Ben took care not only to *be* hard working,

> *…but to avoid all Appearances of the Contrary. I drest plainly; I was seen at no Places of idle Diversion; I never went out a-fishing or shooting… and to show that I was not above my Business, I sometimes brought home the Paper I purchas'd at the Stores, thro' the Streets on a Wheelbarrow. Thus being esteem'd an industrious thriving young Man,… I went on swimmingly.*

People noticed Ben at work when they went home, and he was already in his shop before most were out of bed the next day.

One neighbor commented, "The industry of that Franklin is superior to anything I ever saw of the kind." Another man noted, "Our Ben Franklin is certainly an Extraordinary Man in most respects, one of a singular good Judgment, but of Equal Modesty." No wonder people rewarded him with their business.

THE PENNSYLVANIA GAZETTE

MEANWHILE, KEIMER'S shop lost business and folded—leaving Franklin and Bradford as Philadelphia's sole printers. Franklin jumped at the chance to buy Keimer's failing paper, the *Pennsylvania Gazette.* The only other paper in town belonged to Bradford, which Franklin dismissed as "a paltry thing, wretchedly managed, no way entertaining; and yet was profitable to him." With his talent for wit and writing, he knew he could do better. His first issue of the *Pennsylvania Gazette* appeared in early October 1729 with a jab at Bradford's paper. Franklin announced: "There are many who have long desired to see a good newspaper in Pennsylvania."

The *Pennsylvania Gazette* carried not only news and reports but also lively essays and

Ben Franklin pushes a wheelbarrow full of paper through Philadelphia streets.

CREATE YOUR OWN PAPER

*I*n colonial times, paper was most often made with old rags, creating a thick, heavy paper. As Ben's business grew, his wife, Deborah, collected rags for recycling into paper. He eventually owned nearly 20 paper mills.

MATERIALS

Adult supervision required

- Newspaper, wrapping paper, tissue paper— any kind of scrap paper
- Large measuring cup
- 2 cups hot water
- Blender
- Newspaper (for blotting)
- Mesh screen to match the size of your paper (8 x 10 inches or larger)
- Flat pan with a rim, such as a jelly roll pan
- Old dish towel (for blotting)
- Rolling pin

Tear the scrap paper into small bits and put it into the measuring cup—½ cup of torn scraps will make one sheet of paper.

Add 2 cups of hot water to the paper bits. Pour the water and paper bits into a blender. Blend the mixture into a thick pulp.

Stack sheets of newspaper on a table or counter. Put the screen in the flat pan. Pour the pulp over the screen; then slide the screen around to make sure it is covered evenly with the pulp.

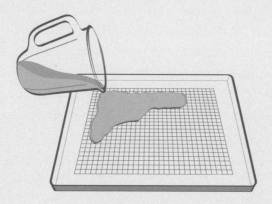

Lift the screen out of the pan, keeping it flat, with the pulp side up. Lay the screen on the stack of newspaper. Cover it with an old dish towel and some more newspapers. Throw any leftover pulp in the trash. Do not pour it down the sink.

Take a rolling pin (you can also use a tin can) and gently roll it over the newspaper and towel. This flattens the pulp and helps squeeze out some of the liquid.

Carefully take the newspaper and towel off the pulp/screen. Put the screen on some fresh blotting paper and let it dry. The pulp can take 12 to 24 hours to dry and turn into paper. If it is a sunny day, you can put it in a protected place outside to speed the drying.

When the paper is dry, carefully peel it off the screen. You now have a thick, heavy sheet of paper to use. You can add thread, glitter, or pressed flowers or leaves to the pulp to make decorative paper.

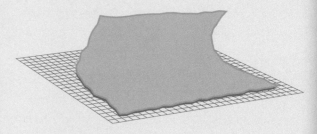

letters from readers. Ben wrote editorials and many of the paper's amusing columns. In one editorial he claimed that Bradford could freely reprint articles from the *Gazette,* but "he is desired not to date his paper a day before ours lest readers should imagine we take from him, which we always carefully avoid." Franklin's essays presented his views through such made-up characters as Anthony Afterwit, Alice Addertongue, and Celia Single. Ben also wrote many of the "letters from readers," taking every opportunity to praise himself and his paper and knock down his competitor! But overall, he kept his paper free of controversy, taking care not to offend potential customers.

Ben's partner, Hugh Meredith, was seldom sober and was a poor printer. His bad habits jeopardized Franklin's hard work. With the help of friends, he bought Meredith out of the business, leaving Franklin with a pile of debts. Slowly he whittled down his debt and expanded his business. He opened a little stationery shop and began making paper.

Bradford's print shop, however, retained one great advantage: Bradford ran the post office. And some customers thought this meant Bradford had more access to news and the ability to distribute advertisements to customers.

"I TOOK HER TO WIFE"

BEN DECIDED marriage offered the best way to control his "hard-to-be-govern'd Passion of Youth." Also, many young men advanced their position in society by marrying young women with money. Franklin discovered, however, that his growing reputation as a businessman did not guarantee parents favored his courtship of their daughters. "The Business of a Printer being generally thought a poor one, I was not to expect Money with a Wife," he wrote. He turned his attentions back to Deborah Read, whom he'd left waiting when he'd gone to London.

Deborah had given up on Ben's promises. She had married someone else, only to discover her husband likely had a wife already living in England. Deborah left him and returned to her mother. The man eventually sailed for the West Indies and reportedly died—but no one knew for sure. Franklin remarked, "Our mutual Affection was revived," and on September 1, 1730, he and Deborah began living together as husband and wife.

Deborah, poor and barely able to read and write, offered Ben little help in his climb up the social ladder. When Philadelphia's gentry invited him to their homes, Deborah did not

Deborah Read Franklin

go. But she proved a hardworking partner, running their home, helping in the shop, and keeping a keen eye on every penny spent— qualities he greatly admired.

Not long after their marriage, Franklin introduced a new member into their family —William, a baby son he'd had with an unknown woman. Franklin doted on the boy and expected Deborah to raise him. Deborah gave birth in 1732 to a baby boy named Francis Folger (called Franky), who died at age four of smallpox. His little boy's death crushed Franklin, who'd meant to have the child inoculated against the disease but had not gotten around to it. He described his son with a few words on the little boy's gravestone: "The delight of all who knew him."

Ben Franklin works at the first lending library.

THE JUNTO

Through intensive reading and conversation Ben Franklin developed his own views of religion. He firmly believed that "the most acceptable Service of God was the doing of Good to Man." He also believed that one man "may work great Changes, and accomplish great Affairs among Mankind, if he first forms a good Plan."

In 1727, while still working at Keimer's shop, Ben gathered a group of like-minded young men together for weekly meetings of the Leather Apron Club. A leather apron, stained, scratched, and worn thin, served as a badge for hardworking craftsmen and artisans. The group included surveyors, clerks, a glass worker, a shoemaker, a cabinetmaker, and others.

Eventually renamed the Junto, Ben's club discussed politics, science, morals, and schemes for bettering society. Each week members exchanged ideas and information aimed at helping one another get ahead in business. Junto members pooled their books together for everyone to share. Ben, a great talker used to "prattling, punning, and joking," quickly realized he learned far more "by use of the ear than of the tongue."

In 1731 Ben Franklin drew up a plan for the Junto proposing the first lending library

❧ MAKE A LEATHER APRON ❧

MATERIALS

Adult supervision required

- ❉ 1 yard of thick, heavy fabric such as denim or fake leather
- ❉ Stitchwitchery or other iron-on fabric adhesive tape
- ❉ Iron and ironing board
- ❉ Scissors
- ❉ Rope
- ❉ Large sharp nail

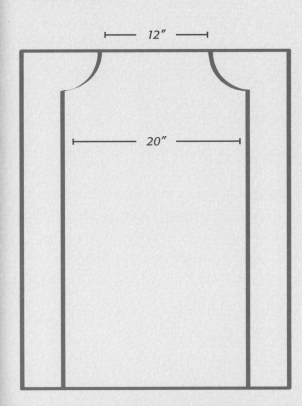

Use scissors to cut fabric into an apron shape (see drawing)

Lay the fabric facedown on a table. Lay a strip of Stitchwitchery along the hem and sides. Fold the fabric over the strip. Iron the fabric. The heat from the iron will seal the hem.

Cut a length of rope about 36 inches long. With adult help, use the nail to poke two holes at the top of the apron large enough for the rope to pass through (see drawing). Pass the rope

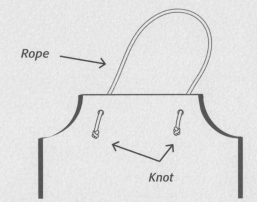

Rope

Knot

through the holes, forming a loop for your head. Knot the rope ends in the front of the apron.

Measure and cut a length of rope to tie around your waist. Now you have a craftsman's apron to work on your own projects.

in the colonies. Franklin described his plan as "my first Project of a public Nature." For a fee subscribers could check out books and read them. The money from the fees covered the cost of buying new books. Years later, as numerous libraries dotted American towns, Franklin noted with pride that the libraries had "improv'd the general Conversation of the Americans, [and] made the common Tradesmen and Farmers as intelligent as most Gentlemen from other Countries."

By his mid-twenties, Ben Franklin owned a thriving printing and publishing business, had married, and had immersed himself in public improvements. He had already advanced further than anyone would have dreamed for a working-class poor boy. But his keen eye for opportunity flung open more doors that he would soon march through.

A Junto Meeting

ANYTHING MIGHT be discussed at a Junto meeting, from "What is wisdom?" to whether or not indentured servants made the colonies more prosperous. Franklin wrote a list of 24 questions for members to keep in mind. A few examples:

What new story have you lately heard agreeable for telling in conversation?

Hath any citizen in your knowledge failed in his business lately, and what have you heard of the cause?

Have you lately heard of any citizen's thriving well, and by what means?

Do you know of any fellow citizen who had lately done a worthy action deserving praise and imitation? Or who has committed an error proper for us to be warned against and avoid?

Hath any deserving stranger arrived in town since last meeting that you heard of? And whether you think it lies in the power of the Junto to oblige him or encourage him as he deserves?

In what manner can the Junto … assist you in any of your honorable designs?

❧ START A JUNTO ❧

For Ben, good works and improving the lives of others was of utmost importance. Gather friends and family and start your own Junto. Have monthly meetings to plan what to do. Brainstorm ideas and keep notes of your plans. Some suggestions:

❀ Start recycling in your home or school.

❀ Walk in a charity race to earn money to aid a cause, or run a lemonade stand to help a charity.

❀ Can you help out an elderly neighbor by raking or shoveling or just being friendly?

❀ Volunteer to help with a canned food drive at your school to help feed the hungry.

❀ Collect books and toys for a homeless shelter.

❀ Write to your congressperson about concerns you have.

❀ Sometimes just writing a thank-you note to a teacher, a firefighter, a police officer, or a soldier can be one of the kindest acts of all.

After you decide on an idea, create a plan of action to make it happen. Contact people to volunteer or find out how you can make a donation to a charity. Ben Franklin knew every little bit counts to make the world a better place!

3

"ANY OPPORTUNITY TO SERVE"

FOR YEARS Ben Franklin sat in his plain clothes, at his plain table, and ate his plain breakfast of bread and milk from a "twopenny earthen Porringer with a Pewter Spoon." He lived by two words, "INDUSTRY and FRUGALITY... waste neither Time nor Money, but make the best Use of both." Then one day Deborah called him to breakfast and he found his meal served in a china bowl with a silver spoon. Deborah made no apologies for her extravagance. "Her Husband deserv'd a Silver Spoon & China Bowl as well as any of his Neighbours,"

she claimed. After the bowl and spoon, other luxuries crept into the Franklin household.

Franklin's business skills and sharp eye for opportunity swelled the family bank account.

His printing business thrived with government print jobs and contracts to print money. He'd become the official printer of Pennsylvania in 1730. His network of influential friends expanded when he joined the society of Freemasons in 1731. Three years later the mason lodge elected Franklin grand master.

BOOMING BUSINESS

❧ THANKS TO Franklin's writing, the *Pennsylvania Gazette* grew into the most popular paper in the colony. In 1732 Franklin added *Poor Richard: An Almanack* to his publishing empire. Franklin believed an almanac offered "a proper Vehicle for conveying Instruction among the common People, who bought scarce any other Books." For the next twenty-five years Franklin published the almanac under the name Richard Saunders, a character Franklin invented. He filled *Poor Richard* with snippets on weather, astronomy, history, and science and included jokes and longer essays. He adapted proverbs that promoted lessons about thrift, modesty, and common sense. A huge success, *Poor Richard* sold nearly 10,000 copies a year throughout the colonies, providing Franklin with a healthy income.

As the years passed, Franklin invested money to open print shops in other colonies.

> ### Poor Richard, 1743.
>
> # AN
> # Almanack
>
> For the Year of Chrift
>
> # 1743,
>
> Being the Third after LEAP YEAR.
>
> *And makes fince the Creation*   Years
> By the Account of the Eaftern *Greeks*   7251
> By the Latin Church, when ☉ ent. ♈   6942
> By the Computation of *W. W.*   5752
> By the *Roman* Chronology   5692
> By the *Jewifh* Rabbies   5504
>
> *Wherein is contained,*
>
> The Lunations, Eclipfes, Judgment of the Weather, Spring Tides, Planets Motions & mutual Afpects, Sun and Moon's Rifing and Setting, Length of Days, Time of High Water, Fairs, Courts, and obfervable Days.
> Fitted to the Latitude of Forty Degrees, and a Meridian of Five Hours Weft from *London*, but may without fenfible Error, ferve all the adjacent Places, even from *Newfoundland* to *South-Carolina*.
>
> By RICHARD SAUNDERS, Philom.
>
> PHILADELPHIA:
> Printed and fold by B. FRANKLIN, at the New Printing-Office near the Market.

The cover of *Poor Richard: An Almanack*

A Sample of Poor Richard's Wisdom

Half the Truth is often a great Lie.

Be at War with your Vices, at Peace with your Neighbours, and let every New-Year find you a better man.

Glass, China and Reputation, are easily crack'd, and never well mended.

'Tis easier to prevent bad habits than to break them.

Beware of little Expenses, a small Leak will sink a great Ship.

A true Friend is the best Possession.

Epitaph on a Scolding Wife
by Her Husband
Here my poor Bridget's Corps doth lie,
She is at rest,—and so am I.

Up, Sluggard, and waste not life; in the grave will be sleeping enough.

Keep your eyes wide open before marriage, half shut afterwards.

Early to bed and early to rise, makes a man healthy wealthy and wise.

Three may keep a Secret, if two of them are dead.

Franklin greets people outside his print shop.

Some of his partners were printers trained by him. He supplied the printing press, types, and other materials. In return, he received one-third of the shops' profits. Eventually Franklin owned partnerships in over two dozen print shops up and down the Atlantic coast.

Franklin established paper mills and may have been the largest seller of paper in the British Empire. He bought land in the West and rented properties. He loaned money and earned interest on the loans. Ben also earned the job of official printer to the neighboring colony of New Jersey. Some estimates place Franklin's income at over £2,000 a year. The average tradesman made about £40 a year, while a lawyer might make £200. Even Ben marveled at his rise from poor runaway.

DESIGN AND PRINT AN ALMANAC COVER

MATERIALS

Adult supervision required

- Large scissors
- 2 styrofoam trays, washed and dried
- Pencil
- Scissors
- Glue
- Newspapers
- Large sheet of aluminum foil
- Water-based block printing ink (from a craft or art supply store)
- Small foam roller or Brayer (a rubber roller for transferring ink; from an art supply store)
- White paper
- Rolling pin

Using scissors, cut the curved edges off the Styrofoam trays to get two flat surfaces. Then use a pencil to draw a design and title for your cover onto one tray.

Cut out all the shapes you want printed. Glue the foam pieces, front side down, onto the foam tray. By gluing it front side down, the design will appear to be in reverse. Let the glue dry.

Place newspapers on a kitchen table or counter. Put the foam tray on the paper.

Lay a sheet of aluminum foil on the counter. Pour some ink onto the foil. Roll the roller around in the ink so that the whole roller is covered. Add more ink if needed. Then roll the roller over the foam tray.

Place several sheets of paper on top of the tray. Roll the paper with a rolling pin, pressing the ink onto the paper.

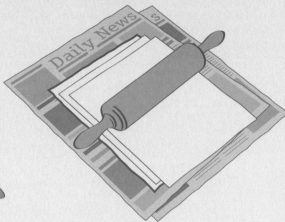

Remove the paper, and you have your print!

"FULLER OF FAULTS"

❧ FRANKLIN WORKED hard, building both his business and his character. He adored plans, lists, and ledgers. On the voyage home from London in 1726, he'd written a life plan, and in 1733 he began a new "Project of arriving at moral Perfection."

I wish'd to live without committing any Fault at any time ... a Task of more Difficulty than I had imagined: While my Care was employ'd in guarding aginst one Fault, I was often surpriz'd by another.... I was surpriz'd to find myself so much fuller of Faults than I had imagined, but I had the Satisfaction of seeing them diminish.

Franklin kept a weekly chart showing his progress living up to thirteen virtues. His chart included humility, industry ("Be always employ'd in something useful"), justice, temperance (not eating or drinking too much), order ("Let all your Things have their Places"), and tranquility ("Be not disturbed at Trifles").

He grappled the most against pride. "Disguise it, struggle with it, beat it down, stifle it, ... as much as one pleases, it is still alive, and will every now and then peep out and show itself.... For even if I could conceive that I had completely overcome it, I should probably be proud of my Humility."

In 1733, after ten years away, Franklin visited his family in Boston. On a side trip to Newport, Rhode Island, he visited his

Franklin reconciles with James and meets his nephew.

brother James. "Our meeting was very cordial and affectionate," Franklin recalled. When James died a few years later, Franklin took James's son under his wing, sent him to school for a few years, and later trained the boy in Franklin's print shop. James's widow kept the Newport shop running until her son had grown. Then, Franklin helped the young man purchase new type. "Thus it was," Franklin wrote, "that I made my Brother ample Amends for the Service I had depriv'd him of by leaving him so early."

FIRST STEPS INTO PUBLIC SERVICE

In 1736 the Pennsylvania Assembly appointed Benjamin Franklin its clerk. He mingled with members of the government and gained a firsthand view of government workings. Jobs for printing votes, laws, and state money rolled into Franklin's business. Sometimes, however, listening to the legislators drove him to boredom. He amused himself by making up math puzzles.

As he built his business and public career, Franklin never abandoned his goal of improving people's lives. Using the *Gazette* to launch his case, he urged the formation of a fire protection society. He wrote out plans,

created rules, and listed duties. The Union Fire Company organized in 1736 with fire engines, leather buckets, ladders, hooks, and other tools to fight fires. Franklin also promoted fire safety, offering advice on everything from how to carry hot coals between rooms to keeping chimneys safe.

In 1737, Franklin won the job of Philadelphia postmaster away from Bradford. The job paid little. As postmaster, however, Franklin vastly improved delivery of his newspaper, allowing him to sell more subscriptions and advertisements for the *Gazette*. "It came to afford me," he noted, "a very considerable Income."

THE GREAT AWAKENING

In the 1730s a religious revival known as the Great Awakening swept the colonies. Relying on pure emotion, preachers such as Jonathan Edwards drove listeners sobbing to their knees with thunderous sermons unleashing the terrors of hell. But Franklin relied on reason over emotion. He felt that few ministers preached sermons stressing what he believed: that man honored God by showing "our sense of His goodness to us by continuing to do good to our fellow creatures."

Franklin did not belong to any church, although he donated money to different ones. He'd kept the hard-work habits of his Puritan upbringing while shedding most Puritan religious beliefs. In 1739, however, curiosity spurred him to hear the traveling English preacher George Whitefield.

Whitefield preached to thousands at outdoor sermons, his loud, clear voice ringing over the crowds. Franklin approved of Whitefield's generous charity work, but standing among the throng,

I silently resolved he should get nothing [money] from me.... As he proceeded I began to soften, and concluded to give the Coppers. Another Stroke of his Oratory made me asham'd of that, and determin'd me to give the Silver; and he finish'd so admirably, that I empty'd my Pocket wholly into the Collector's Dish, Gold and all.

The two men became friends, although Whitefield never succeeded in converting Franklin's religious beliefs. Franklin believed the preacher was a good man and printed his sermons and journals—and made a tidy profit! Whitefield even stayed in Franklin's home when he visited Philadelphia.

One item, however, left Franklin curious. Newspapers reported crowds of 25,000

crammed together to hear Whitefield preach. How could they all hear him? At one of Whitefield's gatherings Franklin worked his way backward until he could no longer hear the preacher distinctly. Then with himself at the farthest point, he formed a semicircle in his mind through the Philadelphia streets and allowed each listener two square feet on which to stand. Franklin calculated Whitefield could be heard by more than 30,000 people.

English preacher George Whitefield

Sally Franklin

IN 1743, Deborah gave birth to a baby girl they named Sarah. Called "Sally," the baby enchanted her parents, who'd lost their son Francis nearly seven years before. Franklin wrote to his mother that six-year-old Sally "delights in her books" and was learning to sew. He wanted his daughter to learn "industry and economy, and in short, of every female virtue." Like most girls of the time, the emphasis on "housewifery" skills meant little formal schooling for Sally. Unlike her half brother, William, who had the best education available, Sally's education focused on sewing, cooking, and running a household. Though Sally never had the quick wit Franklin admired in women, she was affectionate and dutiful and would become, as her father had hoped, "a sensible, notable and worthy woman."

"LET LIGHT INTO THE NATURE OF THINGS"

❧ THE SUCCESS of the Junto prompted Franklin to encourage the study of natural philosophy, or science, in all the colonies. In 1743 he wrote "A Proposal for Promoting Useful Knowledge Among the British Plantations in America." With this document Franklin founded the American Philosophical Society. Franklin's society reflected the 18th century's growing belief that humans lived in an "Age of Enlightenment"—people could rely on reason. They could observe and understand nature. Through this new science of observation, individuals could improve the health and happiness of humankind.

Franklin hoped the society would seek undiscovered American plants, herbs, roots, and trees for study. He had faith that members would find new ways to cure disease and improve learning in many areas, including math, chemistry, the arts, the trades, mining, breeding animals, "…and all…experiments to let light into the nature of things," he wrote.

His first attempts, however, led to disappointment. Unlike the roll-up-their-sleeves working-class members of the Junto, "The members of our Society are very idle Gentlemen," he complained in 1745. "They will take no pains."

Franklin expanded his network of like-minded friends. As postmaster he shipped samples of plants, foods such as apples and melons, turtles, snakes, wasps, and animal skins to fascinated Europeans. He carried on a lively correspondence with many leading botanists, natural philosophers, astronomers, mapmakers, professors, and doctors of the day.

But it wasn't just intellectual gentlemen turning to science. Scientific lectures and experiments often served as entertainment. At private homes and theaters, people flocked to see models of the human body and blood circulating in a frog's foot. They gawked at mechanical clocks and dolls, or the camera obscura, which projected pictures on the wall. They peered into microscopes to view animalcules floating in fluid.

"Electrical parties" were all the rage. Audiences marveled at "The Dangling Boy," whose hair stood on end while sparks were drawn from his nose and fingers. Franklin was "surpriz'd and pleas'd" with the first electrical experiments he saw performed in Boston by Scotsman Archibald Spencer in 1743. Spencer sent mild shocks through volunteers. He caused loud sparks to fly and moved objects

Convicts and Serpents

BRITISH OFFICIALS often rid their country of thieves, murderers, and other undesirable persons by shipping them to the American colonies. Ben Franklin protested against this practice. But he gave Britain a taste of its own medicine by shipping American rattlesnakes to England. "Rattlesnakes seem the most suitable returns for the human serpents sent us by our Mother Country," he wrote, even though "the Rattlesnake gives warning before he attempts his mischief, which the convict does not."

as if by magic using static electricity. Curious and excited by what he'd seen, Franklin was delighted when a European friend sent the Junto a glass tube for creating static electricity. He later bought Spencer's electrical equipment at the end of the man's tour.

"WE, THE MIDDLING PEOPLE"

❧ FRANKLIN WAS furious when Pennsylvania faced a threat from French raiders while the Penn family and the mostly Quaker legislature did nothing to strengthen defenses. If the government would not act, then who would? "We, the middling people," answered Franklin in a pamphlet, "The tradesmen, shopkeepers, and farmers of this province and city!"

In 1747, Franklin helped found the Militia Association to raise and pay volunteer militia companies to defend the colony. The Militia Association would be independent of the Pennsylvania government—a very radical idea. Men all around the colony signed up to protect Pennsylvania. Franklin's local group voted him their colonel, but he turned down the honor and took his turn as a common soldier. Franklin oversaw the borrowing of

The Pennsylvania Stove

COLONISTS USED large open fireplaces for heating and cooking. Not only were fireplaces dangerous, but also much of the heat drifted uselessly up the chimney. In 1744, Franklin manufactured an iron stove that could be built into a fireplace. The stove pulled in cool air, heated it, and then, instead of the warm air floating out the chimney, the heat moved around chambers in the stove, which radiated it back into the room.

Franklin did not apply for a patent on his invention. He believed "we should be glad of any opportunity to serve others by any invention of ours and this we should do freely and generously." Franklin's stove did not work quite as efficiently as he'd hoped, and eventually it fell out of favor.

cannon from New York, designed emblems for the militia companies' flags, and sold muskets at the print shop.

Fellow citizens noted Franklin's cool head and get-it-done attitude in a crisis. Over in England, Thomas Penn—William Penn's son—noted Franklin's activities, too. Who was this upstart Franklin? How dare colonists act outside of the Penn family's government! What would prevent them from acting *against* the government? Penn declared Franklin "a dangerous Man.... I should be very glad he inhabited any other country, as I believe him of a very uneasy Spirit."

CREATE CHARGED CEREAL

MATERIALS
- Thread, 12 inches long
- Piece of dry, O-shaped cereal
- Tape
- Ruler
- Balloon

Tie one end of a piece of thread around a piece of cereal. Tape the other end of the string to the end of a ruler. Lay the ruler on a table so the string and cereal hang down without touching anything.

Blow up a balloon and tie it off. Then rub it on your head or your shirt.

Slowly bring the charged part of the balloon toward the cereal. The cereal should eventually swing up to touch the balloon.

Hold the balloon still! In a moment the cereal will jump away from the balloon. Now slowly move the balloon toward the cereal. This time the cereal should swing away from the balloon.

What happened? Initially, electrons moved from your hair to the balloon during rubbing, giving the balloon a negative charge (–) because it now had more electrons. The charged balloon attracted the neutral cereal. But when the cereal touched the balloon, electrons moved from the balloon to the cereal. Since both objects now had the same negative charge, the cereal jumped away from the balloon, and when you moved the balloon toward the cereal, the two similarly charged objects repelled one another.

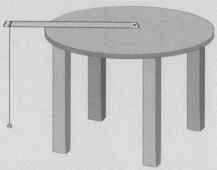

ELECTRICAL WONDERS

GENTLEMEN HAD dabbled in electrical experiments for the previous hundred years. Scientists knew that rubbing a glass tube created friction and static electricity. A French naturalist had sent an electrical charge over 1,200 feet along a wet string. People knew that objects repelled one another when they carried the same type of electrical charge, while those with opposite types attracted one another. An electrical charge could pass between objects. And materials were tested to see what could become electrified (conductors) and what could not.

In 1745 a Dutch scientist perfected a way to capture and store electricity in a jar. The "Leyden jar" was a glass container holding water and iron filings. The jar sides were coated with metal foil, inside and out. People believed a wire through the top of the jar charged the water, though it actually stored a charge on the inside foil surface.

The Leyden jar allowed for a powerful and dangerous shock when discharged. Abbé Jean-Antoine Nollet used a Leyden jar to amuse King Louis XV of France. Nollet caused 180 soldiers clasping hands in a circle to jump in the air with a single shock.

Franklin eagerly began his own study of electricity. "I never was before engaged in any study that so totally engrossed my attention and my time as this has lately done," he wrote to Peter Collinson, a friend in England, in 1747. He practiced his experiments, then showed them off. "My house was continually full for some time, with People who came to see these wonders," he recalled. Like other showmen, Franklin made bells ring, set an "electrical spider" in motion, and made sparks light up a portrait of the king.

With the help of some fellow Junto members, Franklin further explored electricity. He based his experiments on empiricism—that which can be observed. He discovered that electricity was not *caused* by friction, but instead was collected and moved by friction. A static electric charge could flow from one person to another when they touched. He also learned that electricity did not vanish; it was always there in some amount, but it moved from one object to another.

Franklin experimented with Leyden jars, as well. When he dumped out the water and filings, he learned that the glass jar itself held the charge, not the water. He lined up a row of glass plates surrounded by metal, wired them together, and created the first electric battery.

Franklin's experiments dispelled the old idea that there were two types of electricity,

The Basics of Electricity

EVERYTHING IS made of tiny particles called atoms. The center of an atom is called a nucleus. The nucleus holds two kinds of tiny particles: *protons* and *neutrons*. A proton has a "positive" electrical charge (+). A neutron has no charge—it is neutral. Orbiting around the nucleus are even tinier particles called *electrons*. An electron has a negative electrical charge (–). An atom is neutral when it has equal numbers of electrons and protons.

While the protons in an atom's nucleus remain in place, the electrons orbiting around can jump from one atom to another. If an atom loses electrons (which have negative charges), the atom becomes positively charged because it now has more protons, or positive charges. The atom that gains electrons now has more negative particles—it has a negative charge.

Electrons have trouble moving through certain materials such as cloth, glass, and plastic. These things are called *insulators*. Other materials, such as metals, water, and dry air, allow electrons to pass easily. These are called *conductors*.

An experimenter can move electrons from one place to another. The easiest way to do this is by rubbing two objects together. The rubbing builds up static electricity. This happens when there is an imbalance of positive and negative charges.

Interesting things happen when positives and negatives meet! The old saying that opposites attract is true when it comes to electricity. Positives and negatives attract each other. They will pull toward one another. Items charged the same—both are positive or both are negative—will repel, or move away from each other. Charged objects also attract neutral objects.

Static electricity causes your hair to stand on end in the winter when you pull a hat off your head. The hat rubs against your hair, and electrons move from your hair to the hat, leaving a positive charge behind. Each hair now has the same positive charge, so the hairs repel each other. They get away from each other by standing up and separating.

vitreous and *resinous*. Franklin discovered electricity was a single "fluid" that had positive or negative charges that occurred in equal amounts. Today this is known as the law of conservation of charge. Though Franklin couldn't possibly know about atoms or electrons, he realized that "the electric matter consists of particles" so small they could pass through matter. He also created new English words for the science of electricity, such words as *conductor, charge, discharge, electrify,* and others.

As Franklin pondered the mysteries of electricity, he listed 12 items that electricity had in common with lightning. The 1749 list included giving light, having a crooked direction, being conducted by metals, and a emitting a crack or noise upon exploding. Could lightning and electricity be one and the same?

"HAVING NO OTHER TASKS"

❧ As a hardworking printer, Franklin never pushed his place in society. He had never understood the need for a successful tradesman to fall into the trap of "an Ambition… to become Gentlefolk." Movement up the social ladder rarely happened. Everything from dress to manners to speech marked class differences. "People of Quality" possessed education and a genteel air that a lower sort could never grasp, no matter how much money they made.

However, in 1748, at age 42, Benjamin Franklin took a momentous step. He retired from business, hoping to devote himself to good works, public service, and science. In the 18th century, gentlemanly work included

❧ ROLL THAT CAN ❧

MATERIALS
- Balloon
- Empty soda pop can

Blow up a balloon and tie it off. Rub it on your head (or shirt) to build up a static charge.

Place an empty soda pop can on the kitchen floor. Slowly bring the charged balloon toward the can. What happens?

Next, pick up the can and rub it on your head. Then place the can back on the floor. Rub the balloon on your head again. Slowly bring the balloon toward the can. What happens?

Use your knowledge of static electricity, charge, positive (+), negative (−), attract, and repel to explain what happened.

serving in government and looking to the good of your country. In short, Franklin became a gentleman. Franklin prepared for his new role. He'd read more books than many true-born gentlemen. He could talk about numerous subjects. And, he'd even taught himself languages, learning enough French, Latin, Italian, Spanish, and German to get by. He knew gentlemen throughout the colonies, and though Franklin had been a tradesman, these men were used to dealing with him.

Franklin turned over the printing shop to a partner and moved his family away from the business into a new house in a fashionable area of Philadelphia. Writing remained a gentlemanly pursuit, so there was no need to give up his essays, letters, and pamphlets. Like any gentleman in the colonies, Franklin purchased several African slaves. Within a few years he adopted a coat of arms to seal his letters.

As a special sign of his new status, he had his portrait painted, an expensive luxury usually only for people of rank. For his portrait the shirt sleeves and leather apron are a memory, replaced by a dark green velvet coat, a curled wig, and a frilly white shirt with ruffles at his throat. Nothing too fancy or colorful, but the clothes definitely marked Franklin as a new man.

Franklin summed up his new situation to a friend:

I am in a fair way of having no other Tasks than such as I shall like to give my self, and of enjoying what I look upon as a great Happiness, Leisure to read, make Experiments, and converse at large with such ingenious and worthy Men as are pleas'd to honour me with their Acquaintance.

Franklin, dressed in a fashionable wig, points to a stroke of lightning.

Franklin's new leisure time allowed him to devote attention to electrical experiments and social improvements. Most of all, he hoped to produce "something for the common benefit of Mankind."

"FLATTERED BY PROMOTIONS"

❧ FRANKLIN SPEEDILY advanced in Philadelphia affairs. The same year he retired he was elected to the Council of Philadelphia. In 1749 he was named a justice of the peace. Two years later, in 1751, Franklin became a city alderman and was elected to the Pennsylvania Assembly. For the next ten years Franklin won reelection. Though he struggled against pride, he couldn't help feeling "flattered by all these promotions, for, considering my low beginnings, they were great things to me."

Franklin quickly gained power in the assembly. While Franklin seldom rose to speak, he worked tirelessly behind the scenes. He shaped members' opinions and brought groups together. He served on committees, writing letters and responses to the governor. He studied proposals and penned reports. Always ready to promote William's future, too, Franklin got his son a job as clerk of the assembly.

The formation of the Militia Association in 1747 had soured the relationship between the Penns and some members of the legislature, including Franklin. William Penn's sons viewed Pennsylvania more as an unending source of money than the Quaker experiment of their father. Some legislators grumbled that the proprietors should help pay the costs of running the colony. Other citizens paid taxes on their property—why should the Penns get a free pass on hundreds of thousands of acres belonging to their family? Over the next few years, Franklin emerged as the foremost opponent of the Penns.

Franklin viewed his seat in the assembly as a springboard to further improvements. To make Philadelphia's streets safer, he proposed paying full-time professional night watchmen. In 1752, Philadelphia's government adopted Franklin's night watch plan.

For years Franklin dreamed of establishing a school open to any willing young man, not just the sons of the elite. His plans included classes in practical subjects such as writing, math, and accounting instead of classes emphasizing religion and languages. After raising funds, Franklin launched the Pennsylvania Academy in January 1751. Forty years later Franklin's school became known as the University of Pennsylvania. Another Franklin scheme raised money by getting the legislature to match funds from private donors to pay for the founding of Pennsylvania Hospital.

Starting on his own block, Franklin convinced shopkeepers that Philadelphia's filthy streets—piled with garbage, manure, and dirt—hurt business. He submitted a plan where everyone paid a little to hire workers to clean the streets. People seemed pleased with the results and "more willing to submit to a Tax for that purpose," Franklin noted. He proposed to the legislature that city streets be paved, since they were little more than swamps when it rained and were choked with dust when dry. To top off these improvements, he designed new street lamps. A vent in the bottom kept the glass panes free of darkening smoke smudges. Franklin felt that these changes, though sometimes small, contributed to peoples' happiness and safety.

"MADE AT PHILADELPHIA IN AMERICA"

❧ IN HIS electrical experiments Franklin followed the methods of Sir Isaac Newton: science based on empiricism. Franklin's writing skills and organized mind ensured his observations were understandable to most readers, not just the most educated. He and his scientific pen pals always traded information. Franklin sent his electrical observations to Peter Collinson.

Excited by Franklin's findings, Collinson passed the letters on to a London publisher, who released Franklin's writings in April 1751 as *Experiments and Observations on Electricity, Made at Philadelphia in America.* The book

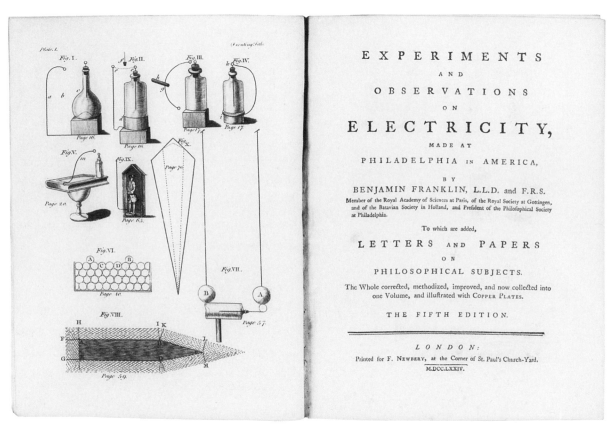

The title page and frontispiece of *Experiments and Observations on Electricity,* 1774 edition.

became a huge success and zipped through multiple printings and translations into other languages. In September 1752, Collinson happily wrote to Franklin, "All Europe is in Agitation on Verifying Electrical Experiments…. All commends the Thought of the Inventor."

The fact that Franklin—a "rough" American lacking education—had written this made the feat all the more remarkable to Europeans. Benjamin Franklin had stepped suddenly onto the world stage.

"LET THE EXPERIMENT BE MADE"

❧ LIGHTNING'S UNKNOWABLE, vast power sparked fires, tumbled chimneys, split trees, maimed, and killed. For centuries people rang specially blessed church bells and whispered prayers that God would save them from "the stroke of lightning, the harm of thunder, the disasters of storms, and all the spirits of the tempest." Lightning remained a mystery, though many people, including Franklin, suspected that lightning was a form of electricity. But how could you prove such a thing? He laid down the challenge: "Let the experiment be made," he wrote.

In 1750 Franklin wrote several letters to Collinson proposing an experiment to test if lightning was indeed electricity. Franklin himself did not try the "sentry box" experiment he designed. A Frenchman, Thomas-François d'Alibard, tested the experiment in May 1752. During a storm, a man sat in a wooden sentry box built on a hill. Atop the box a pointed rod rose 40 feet into the stormy sky. The rod came down through the sentry box's roof. The man inside held a wire that touched the rod. If the rod became charged with electricity from lightning, the man would see sparks. For safety, the wire had a wax handle and the man sat on an insulated padded stool that would not conduct an electric charge. As Franklin had predicted, the rod attracted the lightning and electrical sparks showered down upon the man.

Three days later, d'Alibard reported his success to France's Academie Royale des Sciences in Paris. "In following the path that M. Franklin traced for us, I have obtained complete satisfaction," he wrote. Others in France, Germany, and England performed the sentry box proof verifying Franklin's ideas and d'Alibard's results.

Across the ocean in Philadelphia, however, Franklin knew none of this. In June 1752, he attempted his own proof that lightning was electricity, but instead of the sentry box, he switched to a kite. With 21-year-old William assisting him, Franklin flew his kite into a storm. He attached a sharp pointed wire to the top of the kite. The twine leading down from the kite had a silk ribbon attached, and from the ribbon dangled a key.

As the wind buffeted the kite, the woven strands of the twine became electrified, stiffened, and stood on end. Franklin slowly moved his knuckle toward the key and felt a mild shock. As rain fell, the electricity moved faster through the wet twine, causing the key to throw off sparks. Franklin collected some of the electricity into a Leyden jar.

For Franklin it was not enough to prove that lightning was indeed electricity. Could he figure out a way to use this knowledge to benefit people? Like many others, he had hoped that electricity would provide the power to cure or heal, especially that it might wake "sleeping" limbs. Electrical shocks, they believed, could animate paralyzed legs by removing blockages of "life fluid."

Franklin used shock treatments for "palsies," or paralyzed muscles that would the move uncontrollably. Patients reported sensations of warmth and prickling in their limbs, but the feelings lasted for only a few days. "I never knew any advantage from electricity in palsies that was permanent," Franklin wrote to English physician and friend John Pringle in 1757. He thought people had benefited more from the exercise of coming to his house and the "spirits given by the hope of success."

Franklin returned to earlier experiments with a pointed bodkin (needle) pulling electricity from a charged metal ball. A blunt piece of metal did not attract the charge as

Using a kite, Franklin and William test if lightning is electricity in June 1752.

❧ FLY A KITE ❧

Even before his famous electrical experiment with the kite and key, Ben Franklin made kites. As a boy he once made a kite and let it pull him back and forth across a pond. Franklin's famous kite was made from a large silk handkerchief.

MATERIALS
Adult supervision required
- 24-inch dowel rod or lightweight stick
- 20-inch dowel rod or lightweight stick
- Craft knife (or saw)
- Ruler
- Pencil
- Roll of string or twine
- Heavyweight black plastic, such as a trash bag
- Scissors
- Packing tape
- Toothpick or needle
- Ribbon or old sheet that can be cut into strips

To make the kite, cut a small notch into both ends of each of the dowel rods (sticks) with a craft knife or saw. On the longer dowel rod, measure 6 inches from one end and use a pencil to mark the spot. Measure and mark a spot 10 inches from one end (halfway) of the shorter dowel rod. Then, on a table, lay the shorter stick on top of the longer stick, matching up the marks. This will form a cross shape. The notches should line up parallel to the ground.

Wrap the string tightly around and around the center of the sticks, using an X shape. This will hold the two sticks together.

Pull your string to the top of the cross. Thread the string through each of the notches, pulling it tight as you go around the sticks to make a diamond shape. Go around twice. This makes the frame for your kite. Pull the string back to the X on the sticks. Wrap the string around both sticks again, then tie it off with a knot.

Using scissors, cut the trash bag open to make a large sheet of plastic. Lay it on the table and place your kite frame on top of it. Use the kite frame as a guide to cut out the plastic. Be sure to cut the plastic a few inches wider than the frame.

Fold the plastic over the frame and tape it down in place. Put extra tape at the top and bottom tips.

Using a toothpick or needle, punch a small hole through the top and bottom tip of the kite. Cut a two-foot length of string. Tie one end of the string through the top hole. Knot the other end through the bottom hole. This makes the kite's "bridle." Take the ball of string and tie the end onto the "bridle" about one-third of the way down.

Tape or tie a two-yard-long string to the bottom of the kite to form a tail. This gives the kite balance. Tie your ribbon, or cut strips from an old sheet, onto the kite tail.

Take your kite to an open area on a breezy day and let it soar.

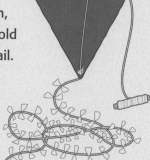

well as the pointed one. Perhaps a sharpened iron rod on top of a structure would do the same. This metal rod could draw lightning from a thundercloud and carry it harmlessly away from a house, church, or ship, preventing fires and damage. Franklin placed a nine-foot rod on top of his own house. He installed rods on the Pennsylvania Statehouse and the Pennsylvania Academy. *Poor Richard* offered suggestions for how to install a lightning rod in an article titled "How to Secure Houses, etc., from Lightning."

Franklin's lightning rod worked—and is still used today!

"THE MIGHTY HAND OF GOD"

☙ FRANKLIN'S BREAKTHROUGH work with electricity earned him honors in America and Europe. One European philosopher claimed Franklin had stolen fire from the heavens. In May 1753, Harvard awarded Franklin an honorary degree, soon followed by one from Yale. The Royal Society in England bestowed its top prize, the Copley Medal, on Franklin.

Franklin's success, however, also brewed controversy. Abbé Nollet seethed that Franklin got credit for work also done by others. Nollet sneered at the lightning rod, claiming it was more likely to attract danger than provide safety. As a churchman, Nollet disapproved on religious grounds, as well. It was "as impious to ward off Heaven's lightnings as for a child to ward off the chastening rod of its father," wrote Nollet.

Franklin dashed off a note to a friend. "Surely the Thunder of Heaven is no more supernatural than the Rain, Hail or Sunshine

Franklin the editor and writer. A Leyden jar and electric dynamo appear on the shelves.

of Heaven," he noted, "against the Inconvenience of which we guard by Roofs & Shades without Scruple." As to the lightning rod, "They continue to bless the new bells and jangle the old ones whenever it thunders," he wrote. "One would think it was not time to try some other trick; and ours is recommended."

But many agreed with Nollet. Who were men to tinker with God's punishing thunderbolts? On November 18, 1755, in the dark of night, an earthquake rocked southern New England. Many of Boston's church leaders blamed Franklin and his lightning rod. They claimed lightning rods channeled God's "resentment" into the ground. A few months later news arrived that a November earthquake had also struck Lisbon, Portugal, killing tens of thousands of people.

"The more Points of iron are erected round the Earth to draw the Electrical Substance out of the Air," wrote Boston minister Thomas Prince, "the more the Earth must needs be charged with it." Boston had more lightning rods than any place in New England, "and Boston seems to be more dreadfully shaken. *O! There is no getting out of the*

Benjamin Franklin. In the background lightning destroys a house.

mighty Hand of God." The use of lightning rods in Boston declined for years to come.

These criticisms did not stop Franklin from continuing to study electricity. He tried several hypotheses, without success, to show what caused electrification of the air to begin with. After experiments in the spring of 1753, Franklin became the first scientist to challenge the idea that lightning struck only from a thundercloud down to the earth. He realized that lightning also sprang from the earth (the positive charge) up into the cloud (which was negatively charged) as the atmosphere tried to balance its electrical equilibrium.

Electricity turned Benjamin Franklin into the most famous American in the world. He changed the study of electricity from an amusement to a science. Yet he wondered what it all meant. An inventor tried to benefit humankind, he wrote, but "if they do not succeed, expose him, though very unjustly, to general ridicule and contempt; and if they do succeed, to envy, robbery, and abuse."

But a little ridicule or envy couldn't stop Franklin's ever-curious mind. Once, when riding with a group of friends, Franklin spotted dust and leaves swirling on the road ahead—a whirlwind was forming. "The rest of the company stood looking after it, but my curiosity being stronger, I followed it, riding close by its side." He chased the whirlwind for nearly a mile, trying to break it up by thrusting his riding crop into the vortex. Not until broken branches whizzed at his head did he retreat. Franklin had described himself perfectly. His curiosity about the world around him was stronger than most.

4

"A FIRM LOYALTY TO THE CROWN"

BEN FRANKLIN dreamed of a grand future for America as part of the British Empire. In 1751 he wrote an essay explaining that while Europe offered scarce land, Americans enjoyed plentiful, cheap land. While the masses of Europe suffered from expensive living and low wages, America's fewer citizens enjoyed higher pay and the chance to thrive. The struggle to earn a living forced Europeans to postpone marriage and so they had fewer children. Colonists married young and raised large families—Franklin himself had been one of 17 children!

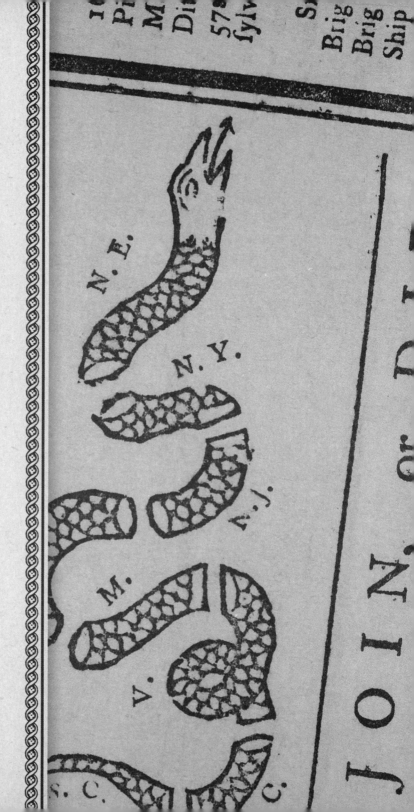

Franklin predicted America's skyrocketing population would double every 20 years, and he proved right. Soon, he noted, "the greatest Number of *Englishmen* will be on this Side of the Water! What Increase of Trade and Navigation! What numbers of Ships and Seamen!" The British Empire could ride the wave of flourishing America.

A CROWN APPOINTMENT

FRANKLIN LONGED for a meaningful role in the British Empire. With the aid of friends he lobbied for a government appointment. In 1753 the British Crown named Franklin, along with William Hunter of Virginia, as joint deputy postmasters for all the North American colonies. Because of Hunter's poor health, however, Franklin undertook the entire job with his usual gusto.

Using lessons learned as postmaster of Philadelphia, Franklin reorganized the colonial post office from top to bottom. He rooted out waste and sharply watched post office finances. He made mail delivery faster and more reliable. Most of all, by 1757 Franklin's business skills had the post office turning a profit.

Franklin placed many of his own relatives and friends in post office jobs throughout the colonies. In the 1700s people did not frown on this sort of patronage but saw it as a perk of office. One of his most important achievements was using the mail to link 13 distinct colonies more closely together. While most Americans viewed their own colony as their "country," Franklin had turned a page. He began seeing the formation of a country out of a union of all the colonies.

THE FRENCH AND INDIAN WAR

BY THE early 1750s both Great Britain and France claimed the rich Ohio Valley as their own. Many Native American tribes preferred the fewer settlers of France to the ever-increasing numbers of English colonists, who were always greedy for more land. In May 1754 troubles began in western Pennsylvania when French forces and their Indian allies crushed a troop of Virginia militia led by a young colonel named George Washington.

Franklin believed France had gained strength from "the present disunited state of the British colonies." He tinkered with plans for a union between the colonies, especially for cases dealing with Native Americans and the defense of the colonies. In the *Pennsyl-*

vania Gazette he printed the first American political cartoon—a snake cut into pieces bearing the names of the colonies with the caption "Join, or Die."

Britain would need Native American allies if all-out war erupted with France. In June 1754, commissioners from the colonies—including Franklin—met with Iroquois leaders in Albany, New York. Franklin convinced the other commissioners that a plan of union between the colonies should also be drawn up.

With the help of Thomas Hutchinson of Massachusetts, Franklin laid out his ideas for the others. His plan called for a council of colonists with a president appointed by the Crown. Their powers included making war and peace with the Indians, raising an army, overseeing trade with Indian nations, purchasing Indian land, building forts, and defending the frontiers. But the colonial assemblies, jealous of their individual rights, rejected Franklin's plan. And in London the king's ministers and Parliament rejected Franklin's plan, as well.

Even with the Albany Plan's failure, participating in the empire's affairs energized Franklin. He hoped the colonists and citizens of Great Britain would "learn to consider themselves, not as belonging to different Communities with different interests, but to one Community with one interest." He even proposed creating two new colonies between the western frontier and "the lakes and Mississippi on the other." To Franklin it seemed clear that the British Empire's future depended on driving France out of North America.

The French and Indian War, part of a greater European war between France and Britain, exploded in the western lands of Pennsylvania. Franklin, a great organizer, rounded up horses, wagons, and supplies for British general Edward Braddock. Braddock meant to capture the French fort at the Forks of the Ohio River. But in July 1755, French soldiers and Native American warriors ambushed Braddock's troops, killing the general and driving the British into retreat. Pennsylvania's defenses lay in shambles. Native Americans attacked frontier settlements. Families fled their homes, begging for government protection. People feared even Philadelphia lay open to attack.

Franklin worked tirelessly for the British cause. The Pennsylvania Assembly passed a bill to raise money for defense, even taxing the lands of the Penn family. The Penns instructed their governor to veto the bill. Franklin was furious. How dare they refuse to pay taxes for the defense of their own colony?

Franklin's "Join, or Die" drawing, published May 9, 1754.

General Edward Braddock failed to drive the French from the Ohio Valley.

In January 1756, the 50-year-old Franklin, accompanied by William and 500 soldiers, traveled to the western frontier to organize defenses and build forts. Franklin also organized a new public militia to defend Pennsylvania and took charge of raising troops. The Philadelphia militia elected Franklin their colonel. This time he accepted. After all, he was now a gentleman. Franklin's regiment, 1,000 men strong, paraded past his house to the silver notes of fifes. A few weeks later the regiment escorted him out of town, the men's swords drawn and raised in respect. Not even the governor or the Penn family received such an honor, Franklin pointed out in his autobiography.

Thomas Penn boiled at Franklin's nerve, "as if he had been a member of the Royal Family or Majesty itself." Franklin heard the rumblings about his arrogance. "The People happen to love me," he wrote to Peter Collinson, though "I blush at having valued myself so much upon it." But if Penn was upset, too bad! Franklin claimed that he had done "more Good in their Country than they" because he had "the Affections and Confidence of their People."

"HOME TO ENGLAND"

❧ THE BATTLE continued in the Pennsylvania legislature over taxing the proprietor's lands. In early 1757 the assembly decided to send Franklin to England to meet with the Penns. Deborah, claiming she feared a sea voyage, and 14-year-old Sally, stayed behind. William, now 27, sailed off on this new adventure with his father.

Franklin sailed not knowing how long he'd be in England. So, after 25 years, he decided to stop publishing *Poor Richard: An Almanack*. On the voyage to London in the summer of 1757, he wrote his preface for the final 1758 edition. Though his usual preface ran one page long, this last one turned into 12 pages.

Franklin, with William assisting, oversees the building of frontier forts during the French and Indian War.

Franklin's beloved home away from home on Craven Street is a museum today. It is the only surviving home Franklin lived in.

Called "Father Abraham's Speech," the piece repeated many of the almanac's proverbs and stories about living a frugal life. Eventually known as *The Way to Wealth*, this became the most reprinted of all of Franklin's writings.

Franklin, now 51, arrived in London as a gentleman, not as the poor printer's apprentice he was on his last visit. The largest city in Europe, with 750,000 people, London charmed and thrilled Franklin. He, William, and two slaves rented apartments in the four-story brick row house of Margaret Stevenson on Craven Street. The widow Stevenson had a daughter named Mary, called Polly. Franklin quickly felt at home. He lavished more attention on Mrs. Stevenson and Polly than he spared for his own wife and daughter back in Philadelphia.

William Franklin

WILLIAM FRANKLIN grew up with the best his father could provide. Unlike his father, who'd spent his childhood borrowing books and learning a trade, William attended the best schools, later studied law, and never soiled his hands with work. Franklin adored William and always wanted his son near. William helped his father with experiments and traveled with him to the Albany Conference and to the west during the French and Indian War. Franklin always promoted his son's career, such as getting him the job as clerk of the assembly.

Deborah, though a dutiful wife, did not adore her husband's son by another woman. One visitor to the Franklin home reported that Deborah resented William and the way Franklin treated him. She accused her husband of "having too great an esteem for his son" over herself and Sally. She once called William "the greatest Villain upon Earth."

THE FAMOUS MR. FRANKLIN

Franklin's portraits were often copied over many times. This portrait by David Etter is based on an original by David Martin that was painted while Franklin was in London.

ONE GREAT joy for Franklin was finally meeting English friends he'd written to for decades, such as Peter Collinson, a merchant and member of Britain's Royal Society, and fellow printer William Strahan. Strahan wrote to Deborah about her husband, "I never saw a man who was, in every respect, so perfectly agreeable to me. Some are amicable [likeable] in one view, some in another, he in all." In turn, these men introduced Franklin to all sorts of interesting and influential people such as writer and scientist Joseph Priestley, physician John Pringle, philosopher David Hume, and economist Adam Smith. Priestley and Pringle became Franklin's good friends.

Celebrated for his electrical experiments, invitations and welcomes poured in. While Englishmen viewed most Americans as rough "yahoos," Franklin emerged as almost a curiosity, making him all the more interesting to English society. He hung out at coffeehouses and mingled with men of conversation and knowledge. People soon craved his image for their parlor walls—Franklin sat for portraits that were copied or sold as engravings. Meanwhile, William dabbled in the high life with the sons of earls and dukes.

❧ DIG INTO YOUR FAMILY TREE ❧

*E*verybody has history! Franklin and his son charted their family tree and dug up information while they were in England. What is your family's story?

MATERIALS
* Paper
* Pens
* Notebook
* Photo album, photo box, or plastic sleeves (from an office supply store)
* Map of the United States, or maps of other countries as needed

Start with yourself: in your notebook, make a sheet with this information—name, birth date, birth location, names of your mother and father, and names of any brothers or sisters.

Now make a sheet for each of your parents. Then make sheets for each of your four grandparents. Add in marriage dates and locations of the marriages, if you can. If any of your grandparents has died, add the date of his or her death and where the individual is buried.

If you can talk to your grandparents, ask them about their parents (your great grandparents).

Once you have collected this information, make a family tree chart (see illustration).

Once you have developed your family tree, go beyond the facts. Interview your grandpar-

ents, aunts, and uncles. What was their favorite movie, music, food, game, sport, school subject, and pet? What was their first job?

Collect favorite family recipes, family stories, and traditions in your notebook as well. Collect old photographs, which you can label and save in photo sleeves, albums, or boxes.

On a map of the United States mark where each family member was born or lived. Did any family members come from another country? Find out more about that country.

For more advanced searches, you can send for a relative's military records from the National Archives. If you know where your family lived, you can go to the library and check census books dating back to 1790/1800. Many cities have newspaper archives online, where you can read death notices and learn additional information.

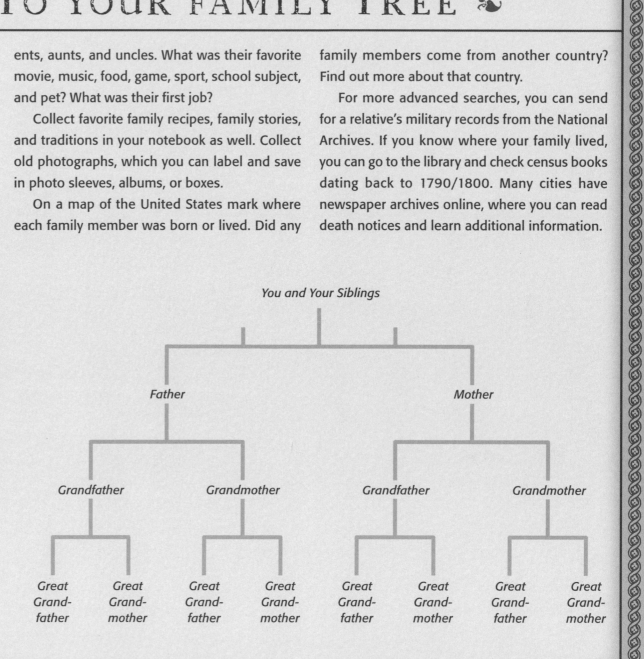

Cambridge University invited Franklin to give electrical demonstrations. He also performed experiments on evaporation with chemist John Hadley. He and William traveled England and visited the Franklins' ancestral home. There they talked to aging relatives, copied information from sunken old gravestones, and dug into their family roots.

In 1759 father and son traveled to Scotland. The University of St. Andrew awarded Franklin an honorary doctorate of law, earning him the title Doctor Franklin. Two years later they visited Holland and met the inventor of the Leyden jar. The Royal Society had made Franklin a fellow, or member, in 1756 for his electrical studies. And in 1762

Evaporation and Cooling

IN A 65° F room, Franklin and Hadley coated a thermometer bulb with fast-evaporating ether. They then cooled and evaporated the ether with a bellows. "We continued . . . one of us wetting the ball, and another . . . blowing on it with the bellows to quicken the evaporation, the mercury sinking all the time until it came to 7° F, which is 25° below the freezing point," wrote Franklin. They learned that summer breezes alone did not cool people. The cooling came from the evaporation of human sweat caused by the breeze.

The Glass Armonica

IN 1759, Franklin heard composer George Frideric Handel's *Water Music* performed on a set of wine glasses filled and tuned with different levels of water. "Charmed by the sweetness of its tone," Franklin invented his own instrument: the glass armonica.

Working with a glass blower, Franklin had 36 glass disks (called cups) made of various thickness and sizes. The glass pieces, each separated by a piece of cork, were strung on an iron spindle set in a wood case on four legs. A foot treadle rotated the bowls. A musician moistened his fingers and rubbed the cups, creating the armonica's delicate, angelic sound.

"The advantages of this instrument," wrote Franklin, "are that its tones are incomparably sweet beyond those of any other; that they may be swelled and softened at pleasure by stronger or weaker pressures of the fingers."

Franklin claimed the glass armonica was his favorite invention, and he had one wherever he lived. He especially loved to hear Scottish folk tunes. Mozart even composed a piece for the armonica. Eventually Franklin's invention lost out to another new instrument, the more powerful piano.

Oxford University awarded Franklin a second doctoral degree—all this for a man with only two years of formal education!

Months flew into years as Franklin enjoyed England. His letters home to Deborah and Sally grew shorter. He seldom mentioned when, if at all, he meant to return to Philadelphia. He shipped gifts, however—crates and barrels crammed with carpets, bedding, dishes, glassware, silverware, shoes, gloves, and fabrics. But Franklin had started thinking about staying in England forever.

A "THOROUGH CONTEMPT"

❧ THE REASON for Franklin's trip was to negotiate with the Penn family, but he had no success. In August 1757, Franklin began meetings with Thomas Penn and his brother Richard. The two men felt insulted, however, when Franklin failed to use their proper title of "True and Absolute Proprietors." The Penns refused further meetings except through their lawyer.

Nearly six months slid by before Franklin met with Thomas Penn again, in January 1758. They argued over what powers William Penn had granted the Pennsylvania Assembly in the old charter. In the end Penn would

PLAY A GLASS ARMONICA

MATERIALS
❀ Wine or water glasses with a bowl shape (use glass, not crystal)
❀ Water
❀ Your finger

Fill a wine glass halfway with water. Clean and dry your hands. Then wet your index finger—your finger should be really wet. Lightly rub your wet finger around the wine glass rim in a circular motion. Keep rubbing your finger around the rim until the glass starts "singing." Can you feel the vibration of the glass? What pitch do you hear?

Pour a different level of water into another glass and repeat the experiment with your wet finger rubbing around the rim. How does the amount of water affect the sound?

Sound is made through vibrations. The friction from your finger makes the glass vibrate. Water makes the glass vibrate less. Less water equals a higher pitch, and more water equals a lower pitch. The size or thickness of the glass itself can also affect pitch.

not budge on the rights of his family. Franklin felt Penn talked, "with a kind of triumphing laughing Insolence, such as a low Jockey." Franklin left with a more "thorough Contempt for him that I ever before felt for any Man living."

Franklin saw only one answer: Pennsylvania must dump the Penns and become a royal colony directly under the king's rule. But only Parliament could dissolve the Penns' long-held charter. Franklin wrote to the assembly in Pennsylvania to petition "the Crown to take the Province under its immediate Government and Protection."

In September 1761, England crowned a new king, King George III. Franklin attended the coronation and proclaimed he saw only "a happy and truly glorious" reign for his new king. He also met one of the king's close friends, Lord Bute, a man interested in arts and sciences.

Perhaps with Bute's help Franklin won for William a tremendous appointment—the position of royal governor of New Jersey. Tongues wagged over how William, an illegitimate son, could have gained such position. As future president John Adams later noted, this "elevation to the Government of New Jersey of a base born Brat" insulted America. Like his own father, William had a son outside of marriage, in 1760. For years

King George III

William hid the boy, named William Temple, with foster families in England.

After five years in England, business interests finally dragged Franklin home. William stayed on for a few more weeks. He married an upper-class woman and in September 1762 received his royal commission.

BACK IN PHILADELPHIA

❧ AFTER LONDON, Philadelphia seemed "thinner of People" wrote Franklin, "owing perhaps to my being so long accustom'd to the bustling crowded Streets of London." He missed the stimulation of London society. He missed living and breathing at the center of the empire. "No Friend can wish me more in England than I do my self," he wrote to Strahan in August 1763. "But before I go, every thing I am concern'd in must be so settled here as to make another Return to America unnecessary."

Soon after his return he set out on a seven-month inspection of the post office service, traveling from New England down to Virginia. Nineteen-year-old Sally accompanied him for part of the journey. While gone, he had Deborah open his mail from England. "It must give you Pleasure to see that People who knew me there so long and so intimately retain so sincere a Regard for me," he told her.

Franklin fell right back into his old role of organizing and running important matters in Pennsylvania. In December 1763, frontier settlers, soon known as the Paxton Boys, turned violent over the government's failure to protect them from Indian raids. They marched on Philadelphia in early February 1764. One night, wrote Franklin, the governor—a nephew of Thomas Penn—ran "to my House at midnight, with his Counsellors at his Heels, for Advice, and made it his Head Quarters for some time." He wrote to a friend that within 24 hours he'd been a soldier, a councilor, "a Kind of Dictator, an Ambassador to the Country Mob." The governor offered Franklin command of the militia to smother the revolt and made him one of the negotiators with the Paxton Boys.

All this made Franklin surer than ever that Pennsylvania should be under the Crown's protection and not the Penns'. Using his influence in the assembly, Franklin hotly blamed the Penns' "tyrannical and inhuman" rule for the colony's troubles. Most of all he urged members to petition the Crown to make Pennsylvania a royal colony.

But Franklin's years away had left him out of touch with many people. On October 1, 1764, he lost the election for his old assembly seat. Opponents accused Franklin of many wrongs, including stealing his ideas on electricity, stealing colony money, and buying his honorary degrees. Enough assembly members, however, still wanted the Penns to pay taxes. In late October they voted to send Franklin back to England and request that the Crown end proprietary rule of Pennsylvania.

ENGLAND, ONCE MORE

◈ BEFORE HE left for London, Franklin wrote a letter to Sally. "I have many enemies," he warned her. She must be careful of her own behavior so others could not use it "to wound and afflict me." On November 7, Franklin sailed again for England. He left behind his wife and daughter and a new three-story brick house under construction on Market Street. Deborah would oversee finishing the home.

Back in England, Franklin quickly settled once more into Mrs. Stevenson's lodgings on Craven Street. At one point he wrote to Deborah that he hoped to be home by late summer. But once again the years slipped by. He would never see Deborah again.

William's son, Temple, had been in foster care. Bills for his expenses were sent to Mrs. Stevenson, who then wrote to William in New Jersey for money. When Franklin returned to London, he brought four-year-old Temple to Craven Street. The boy's identity remained a secret. When Temple turned nine, William suggested his son come to America. William would introduce Temple as a poor relative and his godson, but the boy remained with Franklin, who oversaw his grandson's education.

Mastodon Bones Raise Questions

IN 1764, Franklin received four huge tusks (one six feet long), a segment of backbone, and several giant teeth from a discovery at "the Great Licking Place" near the Ohio River. The remains are "suppos'd to be Elephants," Franklin wrote. They were actually the remains of prehistoric mastodons.

The study of paleontology—earth's oldest living things—was a new science in the 18th century. But the bones, and other scattered discoveries, raised questions. What was the earth's age? Were some of God's creatures now extinct, and why had they disappeared? The earliest discoveries of giant bones had led people to think that human beings had descended from a race of giants that died during Noah's flood. Maybe the earth itself, and the earth's climate, had changed from long ago. Other discoveries included sea fossils found in mountains. Did that mean the mountains had once been under water?

Franklin believed that the bones did belong to some kind of elephant, but he differed with others who thought this animal probably ate meat. He assumed the "elephant" too large and heavy to chase prey and thought it probably dined on plants. Franklin figured this breed of elephant-like animal must be extinct. Surely something this large would have been discovered somewhere if the creatures still roamed the earth.

THE STAMP ACT

BRITAIN'S 1763 victory in the war with France left the empire staggering under a pile of debts. It seemed only fair the American colonies should pay their share for a war that won France's lands in North America. That meant new taxes for the colonies. If common sense ruled, Franklin believed, "You will take care for your own sakes not to lay greater Burthens (burdens) on us than we can bear;" he wrote to a friend in 1764, "for you cannot hurt us without hurting your selves."

One new tax, called the Stamp Act, would tax legal documents, almanacs, newspapers, nearly every type of paper, even playing cards. Prime Minister George Grenville met with Franklin and other colonial agents for their opinions. The agents warned against the tax. Franklin knew it would greatly hurt printers. When Grenville asked for other ideas, only Franklin offered a plan. He proposed taxing paper money instead. This would affect mainly wealthier colonists, who could afford to pay. Grenville rejected this idea, and the Stamp Act passed in March 1765.

Out of touch with American views, Franklin believed Americans would pay a moderate tax. But the colonists wanted *no* tax besides those passed in their own legislatures. The colonies had no representatives voting in the Parliament—this was money demanded without their consent!

To help the colonies swallow the bitter tax pill, Grenville decided the tax collectors should be Americans. Franklin nominated a friend, John Hughes, for a tax collector job and nearly cost the man his life. "The Spirit or Flame of Rebellion is got to a high Pitch," Hughes wrote to Franklin. A "sort of Frenzy or Madness has got such hold of the People of all Ranks." Irate mobs hung and burned stuffed dummies of the hated tax collectors and destroyed their homes and offices.

FRENZY AND MADNESS

❧ FROM NORTH to south the colonies denounced the Stamp Act, even sending delegates to a Stamp Act Congress. The congress denied Parliament's right to tax them. Thou-sands of people charged through the streets. Mob violence, boycotts of British goods, and protest groups ruled the day.

Franklin's printing partners warned that the stamp tax could drive them out of business. While other papers inflamed the mobs, Franklin's papers held to his longtime rule of neutrality. This made Franklin appear suspicious to many colonists. His New York printing partner lost his business, accused of being "no Friend to Liberty."

Some even blamed Franklin for the Stamp Act. One young man wrote, "O Franklin, Franklin, thou curse to Pennsylvania and America, may the most accumulated vengeance burst speedily on thy guilty head!"

In September 1765 a Philadelphia mob threatened Franklin's house. Deborah dispatched Sally to William's in New Jersey for safety, then called on family and friends to defend her home. She and her husband "had done nothing to hurt anybody," she declared. She would not budge from her home. Later, Franklin wrote proudly to his wife, "The woman deserves a good house that is determined to defend it."

The anger and violence stunned Franklin. He hoped for cool heads and actions, "for that is the only way to lighten or get clear of our Burthens." In August 1765 he advised John Hughes that people would soon become

Stamp tax skull—"This is the place to affix the stamp"—adopted in the colonies to protest the tax.

used to the new tax. "In the meantime," he
counseled,

> *a firm Loyalty to the Crown and faithful*
> *Adherence to the Government of this*
> *Nation, which it is the Safety as well as*
> *the Honour of the Colonies to be connected*
> *with, will always be the wisest Course for*
> *you and I to take, whatever may be the*
> *Madness of the Populace or their blind*
> *Leaders, who can only bring themselves and*
> *Country into Trouble, and draw on greater*
> *Burthens by Acts of rebellious Tendency.*

"WE ARE NOT REPRESENTED THERE"

❦ FRANKLIN DID his best to soothe the two countries' differences. He defended America with his pen. He reminded the British public that they enjoyed common goals and economic ties with the colonists. The colonists, as British citizens, had the same rights as the people living in England. To prove his point, Franklin wrote a biting satire insisting the British should force the harshest terms on the colonists. Send soldiers, he wrote, burn their towns, destroy all trade, and kill men, women, and children. "No Man in his Wits, after such terrible Military Execution, will refuse to purchase Stamp'd Paper. If anyone should hesitate, five or six Hundred Lashes (whipped) in a cold frosty Morning would soon bring him to Reason."

Franklin believed that American representation in Parliament might prove the best solution to the problem. He met with members of Parliament, explaining, defending, and informing about the American position. But he came to realize the Stamp Act would

While Franklin's papers stayed mostly neutral, a competing newspaper scorns the Stamp Act.

never work. He also saw the British could not back down.

The great question became who would have the power to tax the colonies—and this was one battle Parliament would not lose. But if the British would just listen to the colonists' complaints and "promise to fix true problems," Britain could "convince and reclaim them (the Americans) by Reason."

In February 1766, Franklin spent four hours calmly and skillfully answering 174 questions in the British House of Commons about the Stamp Act. He said that Americans would never submit to the Stamp Act or pay for any similar tax. Parliament, he said, had no right to lay the stamp tax on the colonies. Yet, Americans looked to Parliament as the "security of their liberties." Americans, he told the House members, would probably not object to charges on imported goods, which were different from an "internal" tax such as the Stamp Act, "which was never supposed to be in Parliament, as we are not represented there." This comment provided Parliament with new ideas for taxes on such imported goods as tea.

In March 1766, Parliament repealed the hated Stamp Act. Franklin's testimony, printed in the colonies, earned him credit for helping rid America of the tax. The British government, however, had also passed the Declaratory Act, asserting Parliament's right to legislate for the colonies "in all cases whatsoever."

For Franklin the repeal showed Great Britain's desire to be reasonable. "As soon as they are rightly inform'd," he had written his partner David Hall, "they will immediately rectify it, which ought to confirm our Veneration for that most august Body, and Confidence in its Justice and Equity." Now the colonists just needed to stay out of the streets and show their gratitude. He shipped gifts home to celebrate. Deborah should have a new gown, as Americans had gone without during the boycotts. "It was a comfort to me to recollect," he wrote to her, "that I had once been cloth'd from Head to Foot in Woollen and Linnen of my Wife's Manufacture, that

Franklin testifies before the House of Commons in February 1766. Not being a member, Franklin had to stand behind the bar.

I never was prouder of any Dress in my Life, and that she and her Daughter might do it again if it was necessary."

"OBLIGED TO BE FATHER AND MOTHER"

Though Deborah urged her long-lost husband to return home, Franklin stayed on, visiting his clubs and dining with great men, even King Christian VII of Denmark. During the summers he traveled with William or with friends, visiting France one year, Ireland and Scotland another.

In poorly spelled letters Deborah poured out news about Franklin's business dealings and life in Philadelphia. Sally became engaged to Richard Bache, who ran a dry-goods store. Deborah agreed to the engagement, as she was "obliged to be father and mother." She hoped she acted "to your Satisfackson," she wrote to Franklin. His reply: don't spend too much money on the wedding. He also believed his daughter might have made a better match.

Deborah seldom fussed at her husband, but now older than 60, she complained that her life was "very harde." In 1769 she suffered a stroke and recovered slowly, stressed by her

husband's absence. That same year Sally had a baby boy named Benjamin Franklin Bache, called Benny.

In 1771, when Deborah spent more than she should have, Franklin scolded her: "You were not very attentive to Money-matters in your best Days and I apprehend that your Memory is too much impair'd for the Management of unlimited Sums without injuring the future Fortune of your Daughter and Grandson." He warned Deborah not to spoil her grandson.

When Deborah reported she'd grown feeble and ill, Franklin reported back about his fine, month-long vacation, "which has given a new Spring to my Health and Spirits." In 1773, he wrote to Deborah that he feared returning to America, for "I shall find myself a Stranger in my Own Country; and leaving so many Friends here, it will seem leaving Home to go there."

TRAPPED IN THE MIDDLE

As the years passed, Franklin watched the divide between Great Britain and the colonies crack ever wider. "Being born and bred in one of the countries, and having lived long and made many agreeable connections of friendship in the other," he felt trapped in the middle. He continued his writings, usually under made-up names, urging fairness and calm on both sides. But the British ministry continued to pass new taxes, such as the Townshend duties, on many products sent to America. Americans replied with renewed boycotts and protests. As Franklin pondered American reaction, he feared there were only two choices, "that Parliament has a power to make *all* laws for us, or that it has the power to make *no laws* for us."

Franklin hoped he might be offered a position in the British government overseeing American affairs. He hoped and waited for three years with nothing to show for it. Meanwhile, Great Britain continued a hard stance against the colonies and sent troops clad in blood-red coats to keep Massachusetts in line. Franklin viewed this as an invitation to trouble.

The Massachusetts legislature named Franklin their colonial agent. He already served as the agent for Pennsylvania, New Jersey, and Georgia. The new man in charge of colonial affairs, Lord Hillsborough, refused to accept Franklin's credentials as Massachusetts's agent, since the colony's royal governor had not approved the appointment. "I have not the least Conception that an Agent can *at present* be of any Use, to any of the Colonies,"

Oil, Water, and Colds

FRANKLIN ALWAYS found time to study curiosities that interested him. For years he'd tinkered with oil and water. While traveling in May 1771, he walked with friends along a large pond. Wind blew across the surface, ruffling the waters. Franklin dropped a teaspoon of oil into the pond. It "produced an instant calm" that extended to "perhaps half an acre, as smooth as a looking glass." After this, Franklin took to hiding a bit of oil in a hollow tube inside his cane. He could then secretly calm the waters as if by magic and amaze his friends.

Franklin also made studies of what caused the common cold. His quite modern results reported that colds were spread by contagion when people were "shut up together in close rooms, coaches, etc.," breathing each other's air. Fresh air, he believed, provided the best defense.

Warming the body with exercise also helped colds. Franklin measured how the body's "warmth generally increases with quickness of pulse." A man walking up and down stairs for a mile created five times more warmth than a man walking a mile on a level surface. Swinging weights also created more warmth. Franklin had learned what we know today—people burned more calories (a unit of warmth) when they exercised.

Franklin lamented. He could not believe how Britain seemed to plant "the seeds of disunion" and perhaps a "bloody struggle" that would end "in absolute slavery to America, or ruin to Britain by the loss of her colonies." He feared British actions might "convert millions of the King's loyal subjects into rebels."

In January 1771, Hillsborough rejected the old petition for turning Pennsylvania into a royal colony. Franklin's mission on that score was finished. Depressed and angry over his failures, Franklin, now in his mid-60s, began writing his autobiography. Reliving his youth and early successes must have been satisfying during those troubled days. In August 1772, Lord Darmouth replaced Lord Hillsborough—and Franklin's hopes quickly soared.

Perhaps he could still foster peace between Britain and her colonies. But then he made a terribly wrong step.

THE AFFAIR OF THE HUTCHINSON LETTERS

THE LIEUTENANT governor of Massachusetts, Thomas Hutchinson, whom Franklin had worked with at the Albany Conference, sent letters to British friends and officials during the Stamp Act crisis. He urged harsh measures against the rebellious mobs in Massachusetts, even taking away "what are called English liberties." If the British did not control the mobs, then "*it is all over with us,*" Hutchinson warned. "The friends… of anarchy will be afraid of nothing."

In 1772, Hutchinson's letters had "lately fallen" into Franklin's hands. In December Franklin sent the letters to a few "Men of Worth" in Massachusetts, asking that they not be generally published. He hoped to show that the blame for Massachusetts' troubles rested on a few people such as Hutchinson, who was now the royal governor, and *not* on the British government in London. The king's ministers did not conspire to steal colonists' liberties. Instead, a few men in Amer-

---

Lightning Rods—Pointed or Blunt?

FRANKLIN'S LIGHTNING rod gained acceptance in Europe, helped in part by armies storing tons of gunpowder in church vaults. One strike of lightning and not only the whole church but also nearby houses could be blasted into rubble. In August 1769 this happened in Brescia, in the Republic of Venice, where such an explosion killed 3,000 people and destroyed much of the town.

Franklin served on a committee that installed pointed lightning rods on the new Royal Arsenal. Buckingham Palace also had a pointed lightning rod installed. Eventually a debate broke out over pointed versus blunt rods. King George III championed blunt rods and had the pointed ones, which Franklin favored, removed. What did Franklin think of the king's change of mind?

I have no private interest in the reception of my inventions by the world having never made, nor proposed to make, the least profit by any of them. The king's changing his pointed conductors [rods] for blunt ones is, therefore, a matter of small importance to me. If I had a wish about it, it would be that he had rejected them altogether as ineffectual. For it is only since he thought himself and his family safe from the thunder of Heaven that he dared to use his own thunder in destroying his innocent subjects.

ica writing such letters to England "laid the Foundation of most if not all our present Grievances." Franklin hoped to cool the hot heads on both sides of the Atlantic.

Against Franklin's wishes, Boston radicals published Hutchinson's letters in June 1773. The furious Massachusetts Assembly petitioned the Crown to recall Hutchinson at once. Instead of reassuring people about the British government, the letters only inflamed colonists' fears. In August the published Hutchinson letters appeared in London, as well. Who had taken and dared to publish the letters of a royal governor? Though Franklin never said how he had gotten the letters, in December he admitted he'd been the one to send them to Boston.

The British Press attacked Franklin for publishing Hutchinson's letters. The *General Evening Post* of January 11, 1774, included the following:

To D____r F_____n
Thou base, ungrateful, cunning
*   upstart thing!*
False to thy country first, then to thy King:
To gain thy selfish and ambitious ends,
Betraying secret letters writ to friends;
May no more letters through thy hands
*   be post,*
But may thy last year's office be thy last.

"Alas! Poor Mungo!"

DURING HIS travels Franklin met the Shipley family. When young Georgianna Shipley wrote to him about the death of her pet squirrel, Mungo, Franklin responded, "Few squirrels were better accomplish'd." Mungo, he said, "should not go like common 'Skugg' with a plain epitaph: 'Here Skugg / Lies snug / As a Bug / In a Rug.'" No, Mungo deserved better. So Franklin penned a poem for the fearless Mungo, who'd perished at the hands (teeth, actually) of Georgianna's dog, Ranger. The poem ends with a political twist.

But, discontented, thou wouldst
*   have more Freedom.*
Too soon, alas! didst thou obtain it,
And, wandering,
Fell by the merciless Fangs,
Of wanton, cruel Ranger.
Learn hence, ye who blindly
*   wish more Liberty,*
Whether Subjects, Sons,
*   Squirrels or Daughters,*
That apparent Restraint may
*   be real Protection,*
Yielding Peace, Plenty, and Security.

In January more news arrived from Massachusetts. A month before, in December 1773, Boston radicals had protested the tax on tea by smashing open 342 chests of expensive East Indian leaves and dumping them into Boston Harbor. Fury engulfed both the king and Parliament. Not only would Boston pay for its treachery, but Benjamin Franklin would pay, as well.

On January 29, 1774, Franklin stood stiffly at Whitehall Palace, in an area called the

A Looking Glass for Ministers

IN SEPTEMBER 1773, Franklin published two satires he hoped would hold "a Looking-Glass in which some Ministers may see their ugly Faces, and the Nation its Injustice." One piece was called "Rules by Which a Great Empire May be Reduced to a Small One." The rules included denying subjects their liberties and rights, sending troops to provoke the mobs, and a "resolve to harass them [the colonists] with novel taxes."

The other satire, titled "An Edict by the King of Prussia," claimed that Britain had originally been settled by Prussians (Germans) and now the English must pay taxes and stop making any goods also manufactured in Prussia. Franklin copied many of the acts that Parliament had made for the colonies and turned them around on themselves. He had a good laugh when some of his friends thought the edict was real!

cockpit. The king's council, the gentlemen and ladies of the court, the archbishop of Canterbury, and any curious members of the public who could squeeze their way in filled the room. They hung on every word and often jeered their support as the king's solicitor general, Alexander Wedderburn, humiliated Benjamin Franklin.

Wedderburn heaped blame on Franklin for the troubles in Massachusetts. "Private correspondence has hitherto been held sacred." He reviled Franklin's character. "He has forfeited all the respect of societies and of men." For nearly an hour Franklin stood emotionless, silent, a man of ice dressed in a blue velvet coat. Two days later the government stripped Franklin of his office as postmaster of the colonies.

But even after his humiliation in the cockpit, Franklin did his best to prevent an

Benjamin Franklin appears before the Privy Council in this painting by Christian Schussele.

open break between Britain and the colonies. He argued against the Coercive Acts (later known as the Intolerable Acts), which, among other measures, closed Boston's Harbor. He worried what would happen if British troops and the colonists in Boston "should come to blows." He wrote to his sister Jane that he would never take "the best Office the king has to bestow, while such Tyrannic Measures are taking against my Country." He waited to hear what the Continental Congress meeting in Philadelphia would decide to do. William, a royal governor, felt torn between duty to father and king. He urged his father to return home, where he would "receive every mark of regard and affection." Franklin expected his son's complete support.

William Pitt, the Earl of Chatham, like Franklin, hoped to reconcile Britain and the colonies. The two men met in December 1774 and again in January 1775, when the earl visited Franklin in Craven Street. The honor of such a visit pleased the American, coming a year after "the Ministry had taken so much pains to disgrace me before the Privy Council," he wrote to William.

On February 1, Chatham presented the case for compromise to the House of Lords. He proposed that Parliament should keep the power to regulate trade and send soldiers but only the colonial assemblies should have the right to tax.

Franklin watched from the gallery as Lord Sandwich rose and denounced Chatham's plan. A British peer, said Sandwich, could not have written such a hateful proposal. It must be the work of an American, he sneered, turning toward Franklin, "one of the bitterest and most mischievous Enemies this Country had ever known." The House of Lords, Franklin wrote to William, shouted down the proposal "with as much contempt as they could have shown to a Ballad offered by a drunken Porter."

Furious at the haste and spite he'd witnessed in the House of Lords, Franklin claimed the group not fit "to govern a Herd of Swine." As the British people and newspapers scorned Americans as "the lowest of Mankind," as dishonest, cowardly, and worse, Franklin wrote to those at home that England had rotted to the core.

Then a letter arrived from William announcing that Deborah had died. Saddened by the death of a wife he had not seen in over ten years, Franklin also mourned his long-cherished belief in the greatness of the British Empire. On March 20, 1775, Benjamin Franklin sailed for Philadelphia, no longer loyal to the empire but an American patriot.

William Pitt, Earl of Chatham, supported Franklin's attempts to reconcile Great Britain and the colonies.

~ 5 ~

SNATCHING THE SCEPTER FROM TYRANTS

O N MAY 5, 1775, Ben Franklin arrived home in Philadelphia. For the first time he'd see the home on Market Street that Deborah had finished following his instructions. He would get to meet his grandson Benny, and he'd brought his grandson Temple home to America. When interviewed by a newspaper, Franklin reported, "We have no favours to expect from the Ministry; nothing but submission will satisfy them." The colonies needed a "spirited opposition."

Most disturbing of all, he learned that while he'd been at sea, the worst had happened— British soldiers and colonists had clashed in Massachusetts, at Lexington and Concord.

The next day the Pennsylvania Assembly elected Franklin as one of the delegates to the Second Continental Congress meeting in Philadelphia in a few days' time. Franklin would be the oldest member of Congress. While many delegates looked to him for his great experience in British affairs, others viewed him with suspicion. Such men as Arthur Lee and his brother Richard Henry Lee of Virginia and Sam Adams of Massachusetts wondered if Franklin were not more British than American. He'd held a royal office, his son served as a royal governor, and he'd worked for years to turn Pennsylvania into a royal colony. Was the old man a friend or a spy?

IN CONGRESS

❧ WHAT THESE men did not understand was that Benjamin Franklin had invested more of himself in the British Empire than anyone in the room had. He'd given his heart, skill, honor, and loyalty, and in the end he'd been humiliated for his efforts. For Franklin, angry and bitter, the situation was deeply personal. But he realized he had to prove himself to many of his fellow delegates and fellow citizens of America.

Never a great public speaker, Franklin kept silent during most debates. In fact John Adams, the brilliant, cranky lawyer from Massachusetts, claimed Franklin spent "a great part of his time fast asleep in his chair." But Franklin served tirelessly on many committees. He helped draft petitions to the king, though he thought petitions a waste of time. Britain had "not sense enough to embrace" the colonies' humble pleas, he wrote to Joseph Priestly, "and so I conclude she has lost them for ever."

Franklin drew up plans for manufacturing saltpeter for gunpowder and plans for protecting American trade, designed new American money, and served as postmaster for the colonies. In October 1775 he traveled to Cambridge, Massachusetts, to inspect General George Washington's Continental Army. The following March the 70-year-old Franklin traveled to Canada to attempt to pry the British Canadians to the American side. The journey, through ice and snow, sometimes involving sleeping on floors of abandoned houses, ruined Franklin's health for weeks.

Franklin's efforts even impressed Adams, who wrote his wife, Abigail, that Franklin had proved himself "entirely American.... He does not hesitate at our boldest Measures but rather seems to think us too irresolute, and backward." William Bradford, the son of Franklin's old printing foe, Andrew Bradford, told his readers, "Whatever was his design at coming over here, I believe he has now chosen his side, and favors our cause."

Franklin still wrote to his many friends in Britain, only now he referred to England as "your nation" and talked about "your ministers." He reminded them of what they stood to lose. America "will not be destroyed," wrote Franklin. "God will protect and prosper it: you will only exclude yourselves from any share in it." Surely "enough had happened, one would think, to convince your ministers

A Family Divided

AS GREAT Britain and the colonies staggered toward war and separation, the Franklin family ripped in two. Franklin's relationship with his beloved son, William, all but ended. Franklin had expected William's support as a dutiful son, but William remained loyal to the king. This embarrassed and angered Franklin. Twice during the summer of 1775, father and son saw each other. The visits dissolved into shouting matches. For William and others who remained loyalists during the war, Franklin was the one who had dangerously shifted his allegiance.

By 1776, William was the only royal governor who hadn't fled America. In June 1776, American forces arrested William. Franklin would not help his son, even though William's wife pleaded for his aid.

Later released, William violated his parole by contacting British generals. George Washington had William clamped into solitary confinement, cut off from the world without even paper to write on. Again Franklin refused to help his son. Eventually the Congress arranged to exchange William for American prisoners. William joined other loyalists in British-held New York.

that the Americans will fight, and that this is a harder nut to crack than they imagined."

Unlike the methods he'd seen in Parliament, Franklin approved of his fellow delegates' hard work, done "without being bribed to it, by either Salary, Place or Pension, or the hopes of any." In fact, members of the Continental Congress faced losing everything, including their lives in a traitor's noose, as focus shifted to gaining complete independence from the British Empire.

THE DECLARATION OF INDEPENDENCE

❧ ON JUNE 7, 1776, Richard Henry Lee rose and proposed a resolution to the Continental Congress. He spoke words that were long awaited by some delegates and dreaded by others:

That these United Colonies are, and of a right ought to be, free and independent states. They are absolved from all allegiance to the British Crown, and that all political connection between them … is, and ought to be, totally dissolved.

John Adams jumped up and seconded Lee's resolution. That sparked a heated debate that lasted into the night, with tempers flaring and arguments flying on both sides. Finally the Congress decided to cool off and postpone the debate. A committee should draft a paper for consideration.

Franklin along with John Adams, Thomas Jefferson of Virginia, Roger Sherman of Connecticut, and Robert Livingston of New York were chosen to draft an independence declaration. Most of the work fell to 33-year-old Jefferson. For two weeks he wrote and revised, carefully choosing each word. After several drafts he asked Franklin and Adams to look the document over.

On July 1, Jefferson's declaration was ready to present. Inside the steamy Philadelphia State House anxious delegates argued, pleaded, and discussed. Franklin's fellow Pennsylvanian John Dickinson urged members to vote against independence. "Shall we destroy, in a moment of anger" the bonds and loyalties "cemented and tested by time?" he asked. In the past Franklin would have agreed, but now he wholeheartedly supported the break with England. As the debate raged, delegates tweaked and slashed through sections of Jefferson's document.

In the afternoon a storm blew up; rain hammered the windows. The Congress took a test vote. Two of Pennsylvania's delegates voted no. So did South Carolina. Delaware,

Franklin and Adams review Jefferson's draft of the Declaration of Independence.

like Pennsylvania, stood divided. New York's delegates held off, waiting for instructions on how to vote.

The Continental Congress's president, John Hancock, as tradition goes, faced the delegates. "We must be unanimous," he told them. "There must be no pulling different ways; we must all hang together."

Franklin replied, "Yes; we must indeed hang together, or, most assuredly we shall all hang separately!"

Those in favor of independence knew the vote must be unanimous on such a great and important issue. On July 2, Pennsylvania's Dickinson and Robert Morris, who in good conscience could not vote for independence, chose not to vote at all. And so the break with Great Britain was made. On July 4, 1776, the Continental Congress officially approved the Declaration of Independence. Church bells pealed as the news spread throughout Philadelphia, and riders carried the word to the rest of the new states.

Now a newborn state freed from British control, Pennsylvania called a convention to write a new state constitution. Franklin was named the convention's president, dividing his time between the convention and the Congress. Franklin urged the new assembly to have only one legislature instead of an

Congress debates independence.

Open the Window, John!

ON THE way to New York, Franklin and John Adams had to share a room. As they prepared for bed, Adams closed the window. Adams reported Franklin as saying, "Don't shut the window. We shall be suffocated." Adams, like many people of the time, feared that night air carried disease. Franklin urged him to open the window and come to bed.

"I will convince you: I believe you are not acquainted with my Theory of Colds," said Franklin. Adams did as told while Franklin explained no one caught a cold from actually entering a cold place. "The Doctor then began a harangue, upon Air and cold and Respiration and Perspiration, with which I was so much amused that I soon fell asleep," wrote Adams.

At least Franklin did not indulge his passion for "cold air baths," where he sat for an hour, quite naked, attending his writings or reading!

aristocratic upper house and a lower house of representatives. He didn't even want a governor. This radical idea smacked too much of democracy. Most of America's leaders were upper crust; they feared rule by the people, seen as mostly lower class and uneducated, and ready to be led astray and wound up into a dangerous mob.

In July 1776 the Congress received a letter from British admiral Lord Richard Howe, a friend of Franklin's. Howe hoped to reconcile England and the colonies. Franklin responded for the Congress, writing bluntly that America could not consider submission to a government that killed its people and destroyed its towns with "wanton Barbarity and Cruelty." Franklin's bitterness seeped through his letter as he told Howe that for his own work at reconciliation he'd been "treated as the Cause of the Mischief I was labouring to prevent."

After Howe defeated Washington at the Battle of Long Island, Franklin along with Adams and Edward Rutledge of South Carolina met with the British general on September 11. Great Britain, said Howe, would not recognize the colonies' independence. Franklin retorted that independence had already been declared; America would "not return again to the Domination of Great Britain." There was no going back.

AMERICA SEEKS HELP

THE NEW United States needed help to defeat Great Britain and win independence. The most promising hope for aid lay with France, one of Europe's Great Powers and Britain's old enemy. Franklin, Silas Deane of Connecticut, and Virginian Arthur Lee packed their bags and headed to Paris.

Franklin in Paris with Temple and Benny.

Franklin sailed in late October 1776. Temple, now 16, and Benny, age 7, accompanied their grandfather.

Better than any American, Franklin understood Europe. He'd traveled twice to France, and his reputation as a scientist and colonial agent had gained him friends and admirers among the French. In 1772 he'd been elected an associate of the French Royal Academy of Science.

Many French philosophers, such as Voltaire, turned to America—seen as a simple place of religious freedoms and social equality—as an inspiration for the Old World of Europe. Jacques Turgot wrote, "America is the hope of the human race, and can become its model."

A craze for all things American swept France. For the French people, Franklin became a living symbol of America. He played upon this image of himself as a rustic philosopher for all it was worth. Instead of a powdered wig, Franklin went about with his own gray hair hanging down and a rustic fur hat slapped upon his head. He wore plain shoes and plain clothes. A Frenchman described Franklin on one visit to the dazzling palace of Versailles as wearing the clothes of an American farmer. "Think how this must appear," Franklin wrote to a friend, "among the Powder'd Heads of Paris."

MAKE FANCY SHOE BUCKLES

*I*n his plain clothes, Ben Franklin stood out in Paris society. Fancy clothes, shoes, wigs, and bold colors ruled in both men's and women's dress. A gentleman wore a long linen shirt as his undergarment. The shirt probably had ruffles at the wrist and throat. He wore long silk stockings tied up with garters. His breeches came to his knee. He would wear a vest or waistcoat. The last item was a long coat with fancy buttons. On his head perched a three-cornered, or tricorn, hat. Men's shoes could have low or high heels; sometimes the heels were painted red. The fashion rage was to decorate your shoes with large silver buckles or even bows.

MATERIALS
Adult supervision required
* Utility knife
* Sheet of cardboard
* Silver paint or spray paint
* Glue
* Silver or colored sequins
* Dark-colored shoes
* Double-sided tape

Cut two 2-by-2-inch squares out of a sheet of cardboard. These will be the buckles. Cut

a smaller square in the center of each, as shown.

Paint the cardboard buckles silver and wait for them to dry.

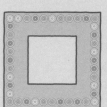

Using the glue, attach sequins to the buckles, either all over or just around the edges. Attach the buckles to dark-colored shoes with the double-sided tape. Now, you're off to dance a minuet at the French court!

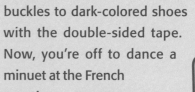

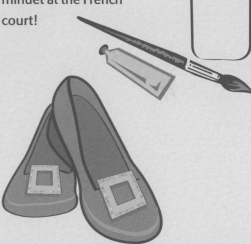

Franklin's life story of a self-made man of common background thrilled the French. One Frenchman noted, "Now one of the first characters in the philosophical and political world owes his present elevated rank in life entirely to himself." Turgot summed up the French flood of emotion toward Franklin:

Franklin scorns fashion for a "rustic" fur hat.

"He snatched lightning from the sky and the scepter from Tyrants."

In 1777, Franklin's *The Way to Wealth* was translated into French and became an instant bestseller. His face appeared everywhere—on snuffboxes, medallions, candy boxes, rings, vases, dishes, handkerchiefs, and engravings. Images often showed lightning bolts. Ladies donned hats topped with metal "lightning rods." Sculptors created busts of Franklin in plaster, marble, and bronze. Franklin wrote to Sally in 1779 that all this hoopla had "made your father's face as well known as that of the moon." King Louis XVI, finally fed up with the Franklin binge, gave a gift of a chamber pot with Franklin's portrait on the bottom of the bowl!

The crowd nearly swooned when Franklin met 84-year-old Voltaire at the French Academy of Sciences in April 1778. The two men warmly shook hands. The gesture disappointed spectators, who'd waited several years for this great moment; so the two old philosophers hugged and kissed each other's cheek in the French fashion to the joy of the crowd! Voltaire died a few months later.

Franklin lived in a house on the estate of a French nobleman, the Comte de Chaumont, in the village of Passy, about a half mile outside of Paris. His house overlooked the Seine River and the city below. At Passy,

❧ COOK A FRENCH FEAST ❧

In the 1700s a French feast offered many courses, including a variety of meats such as rabbit, beef, mutton, quail, partridge, pigeon, chicken, veal, duck, and fish. Salad greens served with oil and vinegar dressing were popular. Sauces starred in many meals, including a creamy white sauce called béchamel sauce.

This French recipe will make dinner for four people.

INGREDIENTS

Adult supervision required

- One package of spring mix salad greens
- Salad vegetables such as cucumbers, radishes, or onions (optional)
- 6 tablespoons of olive oil for the salad dressing
- 2 tablespoons of red wine vinegar
- Pinch of sugar, salt, and ground pepper
- 1 teaspoon of Dijon mustard
- 4 chicken breasts on the bone with skin
- Olive oil
- Salt and pepper
- 3 tablespoons of butter
- 3 tablespoons of flour
- 1½ cups of cream, half-and-half, or whole milk, warmed in a microwave oven or in a small saucepan
- Fresh herbs such as chives or tarragon (optional)

- Loaf of French bread and butter (serve with the meal)
- Several wedges of cheese such as Roquefort, Camembert, or Brie
- Fruit such as grapes, apples, or pears

UTENSILS

- Spoons
- Measuring cups
- Measuring spoons
- Baking sheet
- Salad bowl, small mixing bowl, or glass jar
- Wire whisk
- Medium-sized sauce pan
- Plastic wrap or aluminum foil

STEP 1: La Salade

Put the salad greens into a large bowl. Add sliced cucumber, radishes, or onion, if you wish. Cover with plastic wrap and chill in the refrigerator.

To make the dressing, measure out 6 tablespoons of olive oil, 2 tablespoon of red wine vinegar, 1 teaspoon of Dijon mustard, and pinches of salt, pepper, and sugar into a small bowl or glass jar. Whisk the ingredients together or shake them in the jar. Just before serving, pour a few tablespoons of the dressing on the salad and toss it together.

STEP 2: Roasted Chicken Breasts

Preheat the oven to 350° F.

Place the chicken breasts on a baking pan. Drizzle with olive oil and sprinkle with salt and pepper. With adult help, place the chicken in the oven. Roast for 40 minutes. Remove the chicken and cover the meat with aluminum foil. Let it "rest" for 10 minutes before serving.

STEP 3: Béchamel Sauce

Make this sauce while the chicken roasts. In a medium-sized saucepan over medium heat, melt 3 tablespoons of butter.

After the butter is melted, sprinkle in 3 tablespoons of flour. Whisk the butter/flour mixture together. Stir for about two minutes until it looks light and smooth.

Now, whisk in the 1½ cups of warm milk—a little at a time. Keep stirring slowly until the sauce thickens and bubbles. Let it bubble on low heat for a minute.

Add a pinch of salt and pepper. Add 2 tablespoons of fresh chopped chives or tarragon, if you'd like.

Serve the chicken drizzled with the béchamel sauce. Pass the salad and bread.

For dessert, arrange cheese (*fromage*) wedges and fruit slices on a platter. There are over 1,000 different French cheeses, so be adventurous!

Franklin enjoyed a life of luxury. He had a staff of at least six servants, a large garden to stroll in, a printing press in the basement, and a lightning rod on the roof. Chaumont kept his guest's cupboards overflowing with food and wine. Guests flocked to Franklin's door, and invitations poured in. When Franklin went out, people crowded about his carriage to catch a glimpse before respectfully giving way.

THE MISSION

FRANKLIN'S POPULARITY, however, did not mean that the mission to France ran smoothly. King Louis XVI naturally dragged his heels at openly supporting rebellion by the subjects of another king. Outraged Britain squawked loudly at every turn and threatened France with war.

While Franklin loved and respected France, he faced a great challenge getting Americans to follow. Most Americans knew

(LEFT) French Philosopher Voltaire (RIGHT) Franklin lived in Passy, outside of Paris.

France only as the long-time enemy of England and were divided by culture and religion from the French. The French and Indian War was only a few decades past. Many Americans, including Franklin's fellow commissioners, never trusted France.

With Washington's army retreating more than winning victories, America could offer the French little in return for their help. Lack of news and guidance from the Continental Congress back home also hampered the commissioners, whose ignorance, when asked questions by the French, hurt negotiations and "makes us appear small in the Eyes of the People here," reported Franklin. The commissioners had to master foreign languages and customs. Even Franklin had only a basic command of the French language.

Spies from many countries, including the United States, skulked about Paris—listening, watching, and passing information. Even Edward Bancroft, the secretary of the American delegation, was on the British payroll. He filed hundreds of secret reports writing between the lines of fake love letters with invisible ink. Franklin himself was accused of spying. He declared he wasn't worried about spies so long as he did not dabble in anything "that I should blush to have made publick; and to do nothing but what Spies may see and welcome."

Yet perhaps Franklin's greatest challenge lay with his fellow commissioners. Arthur Lee accused Silas Deane of stealing money and had Deane recalled in November 1777. Franklin defended Deane in letters to Congress. Lee had been suspicious of Franklin for years. "I am more and more satisfied," Lee wrote, "that the old doctor is concerned in the plunder." Furious at his treatment, Deane eventually left America and lived in England—a fact that tarnished Franklin's reputation even more with Lee. And Lee did not get along with the French foreign minister, the Comte de Vergennes. Franklin became the only commissioner the French minister trusted.

Lee and his supporters penned letters of complaint about Franklin to Congress and to friends. Franklin, they wrote, was "not guided by principles of virtue and honor." He refused to sign papers, missed meetings, withheld information, and ignored them. Franklin was "an improper person to be trusted with the management of the affairs of America."

Franklin usually responded with silence. He hated disputes. Plus, he viewed his habits of dining and socializing with the French as a way to win people to America's cause. In many ways, he only copied the French style of living. This was also diplomacy, in Franklin's eyes.

Franklin is presented to King Louis XVI of France.

LEARN FRENCH WORDS AND PHRASES

See if you can pronounce these French words and phrases that Ben Franklin might have used.

ENGLISH	FRENCH	PRONUNCIATION
electricity	l'électricité	lek-tree-see-TAY
lightning	l'éclair	lay-CLARE
king	le roi	luh RWA
kite	le cerf-volant	luh serf-voh-LANT
love	l'amour	la-MORE
hello/good day	bonjour	bone-ZHURE
me	moi	MWAH
dog	le chien	luh she-EN
cat	le chat	luh SHAT
school	l'école	lay-COLE
beautiful	belle (feminine)	BELL
	beau (masculine)	BOH
candy	le bonbon	luh BON-bon
father	le père	luh PARE
mother	la mère	la MARE
Thank you	Merci	mare-SEE
Why?	Pourquoi?	Pour-KWA?
Do you understand?	Comprenez-vous?	Come-PREN-ay-voo?
Do you speak English?	Parlez-vous anglais?	Par-LAY-voo ong-LAY?
Nice to meet you.	Enchanté.	Ah-shon-TAY.
How are you?	Comment allez-vous?	COH-moh tally-voo?
What is your name?	Comment-vous appelez-vous?	COH-moh-voo ah-PEL-ay voo?
My name is…	Je m'appelle…	JUH ma-pell…
Where are you from?	D'où venez vous?	DOO ven-AY voo?

In April 1778, however, Franklin vented by scribbling a blistering letter to Lee, which he never sent. He said he pitied Lee's:

Sick Mind, which is forever tormenting itself with its Jealousies, Suspicions & Fancies that others mean you ill, wrong you, or fail in Respect for you.—If you do not cure yourself of this Temper it will end in Insanity…. God preserve you from so terrible an Evil: and for his sake pray suffer me to live in quiet.

Though the other commissioners thought Franklin lazy, he worked hard. He met with hundreds of people seeking advice and favors. He handled American trade interests, commissioned privateers to harass British ships, and served as director of American naval affairs and as a judge of the admiralty. His grandson Temple (called Franklinet by the French) served as his secretary.

Franklin successfully played on French fears that the United States and England might reconcile. An American victory at Saratoga, New York, in October 1777 helped him convince France that the American cause had real hope. He laid the groundwork for France's committing not only money and weapons but also its own military strength to the American war.

Alarmed, the British reached out, offering the colonies everything but independence. As a prod to the French, Franklin met with a British agent. The tactic worked. In February 1778, Franklin achieved the most important stroke of diplomacy in American history. He signed two treaties with the French—one was a trade agreement, and the other pledged France's military might to aid the United States.

To the landmark treaty signing, Franklin wore an old blue velvet coat. When asked why he dressed this way, he replied, "to give it a little revenge. I wore this Coat on the day Wedderburn abused me at Whitehall."

JOHN ADAMS IS SHOCKED

❧ CONGRESS REPLACED Silas Deane with John Adams, who arrived in Paris in April 1778. A brilliant lawyer and advocate for independence, Adams had few diplomatic bones in his body. In France he often appeared awkward, outspoken, and usually irritated with Franklin. Adams thought Franklin too old, too infirm, and too lazy "to be sufficient for the Discharge of all the important Duties." He felt Franklin did not take the mission seriously.

Arthur Lee and Franklin did not get along in Paris.

Adams's ire rose as Franklin stayed out late and flirted with bold women. The flirting shocked Adams, who reported in disgust that Franklin's neighbor, Anne-Louise de Harancourt Brillon de Jouy, called the old man "cher Papa," sat on Franklin's lap, and flirted, even in front of her husband. This was too much for Adams's Puritan upbringing.

It also irked Adams that Franklin was beloved and given all the credit for the commissioners' work. Still miffed years later, Adams would write:

The History of our Revolution will be one continued Lye from one end to the other. The essence of the whole will be that Dr. Franklin's electrical Rod smote the Earth and out sprung General Washington. That Franklin electrified him with his rod—and thence forward these two conducted all the Policy, Negotiations, Legislatures and War.

Franklin always tried to stay above arguments and now shrugged off Adams's complaints. "Somebody, it seems, gave out that I lov'd Ladies," he wrote, "and then every body

Franklin watches the signing of the Treaty of Alliance between the United States and France.

presented me their Ladies (or the Ladies presented themselves) to be embrac'd, that is to have their Necks kiss'd. For as to kissing of Lips or Cheeks it is not the Mode here; the first is reckon'd rude, & the other may rub off the Paint (makeup)."

Franklin was much harder on his daughter than the French ladies. Though Sally wrote how she made her own clothes, even spinning and weaving the cloth, Franklin claimed she "disgusted" him by also asking him to send such "foolish luxuries" as long, black pins, lace, and feathers. Instead, he wrote, if she wore her old clothes and did not mend the holes "they will come in time to be lace; and feathers, my dear girl, may be had in America from every cock's tail." He did heartily approve, however, when Sally helped organize, cut, and sew 2,000 shirts for Washington's army.

MINISTER TO FRANCE

❧ IN SEPTEMBER 1778, with the American commissioners barely speaking to one another, Congress recalled Lee and Adams, leaving Franklin as the sole minister. Lee continued to badmouth Franklin to Congress, but pressure from the French decided

Franklin's popularity with the French often irritated his fellow commissioners. Here he is crowned with a laurel wreath.

the issue—Franklin was the man they wanted in Paris.

In 1781, after Congress had sent John Laurens of South Carolina to negotiate a new loan from France, Franklin asked Congress for a vote of confidence. They reaffirmed Franklin's appointment, but he burned at the lack of gratitude for his hard work—achieving the treaties and gaining millions of livres in loans from the French. Why did Congress think "that France has Money enough for all her Occasions and all ours besides; and that if she does not supply us, it is owing to her Want of Will, or to my Negligence."

He also had to keep the account books carefully so that Congress did not overdraw on the loans. "The Storm of Bills..." Franklin wrote to John Jay in Spain, "has terrified

"Dialogue Between the Gout and Mr. Franklin"

BEN FRANKLIN suffered from gout, a form of arthritis that attacked the joints. A painful, burning, swollen gout attack lasted from five to ten days. At midnight on October 22, 1780, Franklin was up suffering and penned a chat between himself and his gout.

Franklin cries out in pain:

Eh! Oh! Eh! What have I done to merit these cruel sufferings?

The Gout: *Many things; you have ate and drank too freely, and too much indulged those legs of yours in their indolence (laziness).*

Mr. F: *Who is it that accuses me?*

The Gout: *It is I, even I, the Gout.*

Mr. F: *What! My enemy in person?*

The Gout: *No, not your enemy.*

Mr. F: *I repeat it, my enemy; for you would not only torment my body to death, but ruin my good name; you reproach me as a glutton and a tippler (drinker); now all the world, that knows me, will allow that I am neither the one nor the other.*

The Gout: *The world may think as it pleases... but I very well know that the quantity of meat and drink proper for a man who takes a reasonable degree of exercise, would be too much for another who never takes any.*

Mr. F: *I take—eh! Oh!—as much exercise—eh!—as I can, Madam Gout. You know my sedentary state, and on that account, it would seem, Madam Gout, as if you might spare me a little, seeing it is not altogether my own fault.*

The Gout: *...You ought to walk or ride; or if the weather prevents that, play at billiards. But let us examine your course of life. While the mornings are long, and you have leisure to go abroad, what do you do? Why, instead of gaining an appetite for breakfast by... exercise, you amuse yourself with books, pamphlets, or newspapers, which commonly are not worth the reading.... I have a good number of twinges for you tonight, and you may be sure of some more tomorrow.... Do you remember how often you have promised yourself... a walk... and have violated your promise, alleging at one time, it was too cold, at another too warm, too windy, too moist, or what else you please; when in truth it was too nothing but your... love of ease?*

Mr. F: *That I confess may have happened occasionally....*

The Gout: *Your confession is very far short of the truth; the gross amount is one hundred and ninety-nine times.*

Mr. F: *Is it possible?*

Even the brilliant and reasonable Mr. Franklin did not win his argument with Madam Gout!

and vexed me to such a Degree that I have been depriv'd of Sleep." He wrote to Robert Morris, head of finance, not to expect thanks for Morris's service. You will be "censured by malevolent cricks and Bug Writers, who will abuse you while you are serving them and wound your Character." These critics, wrote Franklin, were like "those little dirty stinking insects… molesting & wounding us while our Sweat & Blood is contributing to their Subsistence."

John Adams returned to Paris in 1780 with the authority to negotiate peace with Great Britain, but Britain squashed that idea. Franklin sighed that Adams would now poke his nose into the supposed "defects" of Franklin's own negotiations with the French. Adams saw the Comte de Vergennes as an enemy—"to think of Gratitude to France," he wrote, "is the greatest of Follies." Adams insulted the French foreign minister, and Vergennes complained to Franklin, much to the American's embarrassment. Adams, noted Franklin, "is always an honest Man, often a wise one, but sometimes… absolutely out of his senses."

In June 1781 Congress created a commission to open peace negotiations again with Britain. Franklin, Adams, and John Jay would carry out the work. Franklin hoped "the ravings of a certain mischievous Mad-man (Adams) here against France and its Ministers, which I hear every Day will not be regarded in America." Why couldn't people understand that this hard line toward France did "irreparable harm" to America? Why wasn't America more grateful to France, who had sent weapons, money, armies, and its navy to aid the American cause? The war eventually cost France over a billion livres.

John Adams

PEACE TREATY!

❧ FRANKLIN'S RESPECT for France, however, did not stop him from going along with Adams and Jay and making a separate peace with Great Britain that left France in the cold. On November 30, 1782, Franklin, Adams, Jay, and Henry Laurens signed a preliminary peace treaty with Great Britain. In it Britain recognized American independence. The new country's borders would stretch to the Mississippi River in the west and from the Great Lakes in the north to the 31st parallel in the south (near present-day Jacksonville, Florida). Congress would recommend that the states restore the property of loyalists. Franklin had compromised on this point. He believed loyalists should not be repaid for their losses unless patriots, too, were paid for the looting, burning, and destruction of war that ruined their lives.

It fell to Franklin to explain and apologize to Vergennes for going behind France's back. Franklin stressed America's love for and gratitude to France and King Louis XVI. No final peace would take place until France and England had also come to terms. He claimed that the British "flatter themselves they have already divided us." Franklin hoped the British "will find themselves totally mistaken."

Franklin even requested another loan. He hoped to never again have to ask for more money. He knew the "enormous Expense" the war had cost France. Vergennes grumbled, "We shall be but poorly paid for all that we have done for the United States." But there was little he could do. He agreed to Franklin's request for yet again more money.

Franklin and the other peace commissioners signed the final treaty in September 1783. "I hope it will be lasting," wrote Franklin, "for in my opinion, there never was a good war or a bad peace." The regard of the French

The Comte de Vergennes, French foreign minister

people for Franklin, and his personal connection with France, had allowed him to achieve diplomatic success against all odds. Franklin alone had kept the alliance going for over six years, granting the struggling United States the chance to defeat one of the Great Powers of the world. A new nation had been born.

Peace within Franklin's own family came harder. After the war William wrote to his father, asking that they, too, make peace. Franklin replied, "Indeed, nothing has ever hurt me so much and affected me with such Sensations, as to find my self deserted in my old Age by my only son; and not only deserted, but to find him taking up Arms against me, in a Cause wherein my good Fame, fortune and Life were all at Stake." When William said he'd owed loyalty to his king and country, Franklin snapped back, "There are Natural Duties which precede political Ones, and cannot be extinguished by them."

The two men met several times, dealing mostly with financial affairs and Temple's inheritance. But the war had severed their close bond forever. In his will Franklin left William some poor land in Nova Scotia and

The American peace commissioners, John Jay, John Adams, Benjamin Franklin, Henry Laurens, plus William Temple. The British commissioners refused to sit for the Benjamin West painting, so it was never finished.

books that William already had. "The part he acted against me in the late war," stated Franklin, "which is of public Notoriety will account for my leaving him no more of an Estate he endeavored to deprive me of."

95

6

"SOMETHING FIT TO END WITH"

B ENJAMIN FRANKLIN stayed on in Paris at the end of the American Revolution. The Congress had not recalled him, so he remained, enjoying life in France while he continued diplomacy on America's behalf. Franklin's reputation in Europe helped gain recognition for the United States as it sought its place among the nations of the world. While still in Paris, Franklin led negotiations for treaties between the new United States of America and Prussia and Sweden.

Benny returned to Passy after four years at school in Geneva, Switzerland. Franklin taught his grandson to swim, and Temple taught his 14-year-old cousin how to fence and dance. Benny also began learning how to use Franklin's printing press at Passy.

John Adams, back in France with his wife, Abigail, remained amazed at France's love for Franklin. The French women's "unaccountable passion for old age" especially shocked Adams, who noted how they buzzed around Franklin. Franklin seemed to have a crush on Anne-Catherine Helvétius, a widow who hosted salons with the most entertaining, witty, and brilliant people in Paris. Franklin, half in play, often asked Madame Helvétius to marry him. The Adamses thought the woman bold and loose. She threw her arms about people and sprawled in an unladylike manner on the sofa, "where she shew more than her feet," wrote Abigail in September 1784.

The flood of Europeans to America, which they viewed as a place to get rich quickly, continually annoyed Franklin. For his taste, too many of them "value themselves and expect to be valued by us for their Birth or Quality, though I tell them those things bear no Price in our Markets." If Franklin had his way, only people with a "useful Trade or Art by which they may get a living" would sail across the Atlantic.

Finally, fed up with repeating himself, Franklin wrote a pamphlet in February 1784 that was packed with information and titled *Those Who Would Remove to America*. Franklin warned that while America's acres might be cheap, the land required hard work to make a living. America, he said, was the "Land of Labour." And no cushy government jobs, like the elite expected in European nations, waited for them in America. In America, wrote Franklin, people did not ask, "What IS he? but What can he DO?"

THE BALLOON CRAZE

❧ ON JUNE 4, 1783, Franklin witnessed the first successful attempts by humans to soar above the earth. Two brothers, Michel and Jacques-Étienne Montgolfier, tested an unmanned hot-air balloon. In August, Franklin along with about 50,000 others watched another unmanned balloon flight by Jacques Charles. This balloon used hydrogen gas (discovered in 1766) instead of hot air to lift it into the sky. The silk balloon, which measured 12 feet in diameter, landed in a village 15 miles away! "It diminish'd in Appar-

A copy of Charles Wilson Peale's portrait of Franklin, around 1785–87. Peale's portrait clearly shows Franklin's bifocals.

ent Magnitude as it rose," Franklin wrote to a friend at the Royal Society, "till it enter'd the Clouds, when it seemed to me scarce bigger than an Orange, and soon after became invisible, the Clouds concealing it."

A balloon craze swept France, and Franklin, too. In September the Montgolfiers staged another flight at Versailles in front of the royal family and 130,000 Parisians. On board traveled the first balloon passengers—a sheep, a duck, and a rooster. All creatures landed safely but, unfortunately, could not report about their experiences.

The first manned flight occurred on November 21. The two men onboard waved their hats to spectators, including Franklin. The spectators "had great Pleasure in seeing the Adventurers go off so cheerfully, and applauded them," wrote Franklin, "but there was at the same time a good deal of Anxiety for their Safety." The balloon traveled 20 minutes before a gentle landing, to the popping of champagne corks. The next day the Montgolfiers visited Franklin at his home, where he signed an official certificate of the historic manned flight. "Nothing is wanted," wrote Franklin, "but some light handy Instruments to give and direct Motion."

Two weeks later 400,000 people crushed together to watch another manned flight. "Never before was a philosophical (science)

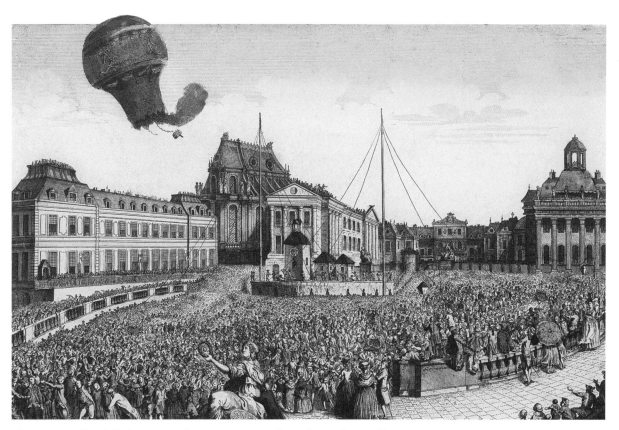

The Montgolfiers' flight, September 19, 1783, at the Palace of Versailles.

Larger in America

FRANKLIN BELIEVED that Americans were growing larger than Europeans. At a dinner party in Paris he asked everyone at the table to stand up. Every American towered over the French citizens. One guest recalled, "There was not one American present who could not have tost out of the Windows any one or perhaps two of the rest of the Company."

experiment so magnificently attended," gushed Franklin. A wicker basket beneath the balloon held a small table so the three passengers could make notes and for the first time describe what the earth and clouds looked like from high above.

"A few months [ago] the idea of Witches riding thro' the Air upon a Broomstick, and that of Philosophers upon a Bag of Smoke, would have appear'd equally impossible and ridiculous," noted Franklin. For centuries man had dreamed of flying—and now it had come true! In January the first British ballooning attempts took place.

Surprised citizens in a French village inspect a fallen balloon.

THE AUTOBIOGRAPHY, PART TWO

❧ THE FIRST part of Franklin's autobiography covered his early life. He'd written it in England during a time of uncertainty and frustration. Franklin gave the pages to his friend Joseph Galloway. But Galloway, a loyalist during the war, fled America. The writings turned up in the hands of Mrs. Galloway's lawyer, Abel James. James urged Franklin to continue the work, so "useful & entertaining not only to a few, but to millions." An English friend seconded these thoughts. "Your life is so remarkable, that if you do not give it, somebody else will," wrote Benjamin Vaughan to Franklin. Just think, said Vaughan, how Franklin's words might inspire a future generation of great and wise men.

How could Franklin resist these arguments? He began writing, this time creating a plan for achieving happiness and success, different from the chatty stories of the biography's first half. He believed that his successful mission in France and the treaty with Great Britain had proved his theory that a few men of good judgment and common sense could "work great Change, and accomplish great Affairs among mankind."

MESMERIZED!

☙ In 1778 a German native named Friedrich Mesmer arrived in Paris. Mesmer claimed he had powers to control a healing magnetic force, allowing him to cure paralysis, eye troubles, blocked intestines, anxiety, and depression. By "mesmerizing," or touching patients with his hands or an iron wand or rod, Mesmer removed a blockage that stopped the flow of the body's "magnetic fluids." At Mesmer's touch, patients trembled and convulsed, the blockage moved, the magnetic fluid flowed, and the patient recovered. Mesmer opened several clinics and also held healing gatherings for entire rooms of patients.

When compared with typical "heroic" treatments of the day—bleeding, purging, blistering, harsh tonics, and electrical shocks—Mesmer's treatments seemed gentle. He even had Franklin's armonica played during treatments for the otherworldly sound. The ill and infirm flocked to Mesmer's mass healings. He soon trained other "mesmerists," and branches of his clinics popped up all over France.

But Mesmer had not won over France's scientists or physicians. His followers asked why the idea of a magnetic flow in the body should seem stranger than Newton's claims of gravity or Franklin's claim to pull light-

ning from the skies. Temple belonged to one of Mesmer's "Harmony Societies."

Franklin believed many people "are never in health, because they are fond of Medicines." They ruined their health through this love of treatments. "If these people can be persuaded to forbear their Drugs in Expectation of being cured by one of the Physician's

Bifocals

AS FRANKLIN aged, his eyesight grew worse. He constantly switched between two pairs of glasses, one to see close-up and one to see at a distance. One evening at dinner he grew especially frustrated. He either couldn't see his plate or couldn't read the expressions of the other guests across the table. So he devised a solution to his problem.

Franklin cut the lenses of two separate pairs of glasses into semicircular halves. Then he combined the lenses. "By this means, as I wear my spectacles constantly, I have only to move my Eyes up or down as I want to see distinctly far or near, the proper glasses being always ready," he wrote to a friend. Even Franklin was surprised at this easy solution. "If all the other Defects and Infirmities," he wrote, "were as easily and cheaply remedied, it would be worth while for Friends to live a good deal longer." Bifocal lenses are still in use today.

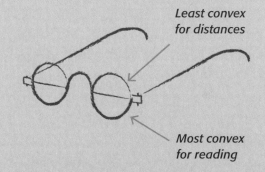

Least convex for distances

Most convex for reading

Franklin drew a rough sketch, like this one, of his bifocals in a letter to a friend.

The Turkey and the Eagle

IN A January 1784 letter to Sally, Franklin humorously expressed his views about the bald eagle serving as an emblem to the country. "I wish the Bald Eagle had not been chosen as the Representative of our Country; he is a Bird of bad moral character; he does not get his living honestly" but instead steals food from others. "For in Truth, the Turk'y is in comparison a much more respectable Bird, and withal a true original Native of America. Eagles have been found in all Countries, but the Turk'y was peculiar to ours.... He is, though a little vain and silly,... a Bird of Courage" who "would not hesitate to attack a Grenadier of the British Guards, who should presume to invade his Farm Yard with a *red* Coat on."

Fingers or an Iron Rod pointing at them, they may possibly find good Effects tho' they mistake the Cause."

In 1784 the Academy of Sciences set up a committee to investigate Mesmer's claims. Franklin served as a member and offered his garden at Passy to test Mesmer's theories. Blindfolded patients thought mesmerists treated them, but they were actually treated by committee members using Mesmer's words and gestures. The patients claimed they felt the magnetic fluids flowing. Meanwhile, real mesmerists "magnetized" subjects without their knowledge. These patients felt no effect of the magnetic fluids. The committee kept a boy in Franklin's house while a mesmerist magnetized a tree. The boy was told to find the tree. He went into convulsions and passed out after hugging a non-magnetized tree.

The committee concluded that no magnetic fluid existed and that Mesmer's effects came from the patient's imagination or from copying others. They labeled Mesmer a fraud who preyed on people, especially women, who were seen as more emotional and weak. A cartoon showed Franklin leading a charge of committee members waving their report as Mesmer fled on a broomstick.

Magnetism, however, was "a science which is still brand new" that needed further study, as well as "the influence of the psychological on the physical," reported the committee. Mesmer left Paris in 1785 and roamed Europe defending his methods. The word *mesmerize*, meaning to hypnotize, comes from Friedrich Mesmer's name and treatment.

AU REVOIR TO FRANCE

IN MAY 1785, Franklin finally heard from Congress that his mission was over. They had named Thomas Jefferson America's new minister to France. Franklin began packing for the journey back to Philadelphia, having spent nine happy years in Paris. "If I had no country of my own it would be Paris where I should like to finish out my days," he wrote, "but I want to enjoy for a moment the pleasure of seeing my fellow citizens free and ready for all the happiness I wish them."

While packing, Franklin opened the door to a young man from Holland who had come to show evidence from his electrical experiments to the Academy of Sciences. Martinus van Marum worked at a museum with a large "electrical friction machine" the young man had designed. It took four people to crank, and it generated electrical sparks two feet long with veinlike branches much like lightning.

"This venerable old man, whose presence inspired me with such profound respect, made me sit down beside him," wrote van Marum. Franklin studied the plans and images van Marum had brought. Did this accurately show electrical exchanges? Franklin asked. It did. "This then proves my theory of a single electric fluid, and it is now high time to reject the theory of two sorts of fluid." Then Franklin excused himself to finish packing.

Out of the previous 27 years, Franklin had spent only three and half years in America. His friends in America were dying off. "I have been so long abroad," he wrote to his son William, that "I should now be almost a Stranger in my own Country." He'd been hurt by challenges to his patriotism from fellow commissioners and members of Congress. Some Americans wondered whether Franklin's loyalties lay more with France or his new nation.

Franklin wanted Temple, the "Son who makes up to me my Loss by the Estrangement of his Father," to deliver the peace treaty to Congress. But the honor went to a friend of John Adams. Franklin asked Congress to name his 24-year-old grandson to a new commission seeking trade treaties with Europe. Most of all he wished to see Temple

DESIGN A TURKEY SEAL FOR THE UNITED STATES

*W*e've all seen the eagle on the national seal. A banner held in his beak proclaims E Pluribus Unum ("Out of Many, One"), a motto that Franklin proposed. The eagle's talons grasp an olive branch with 13 leaves on one side and 13 arrows on the other. The number 13 represents the original 13 states. A shield with stripes covers the bird's body. But what if Franklin's jest had won out?

MATERIALS

Adult supervision required

- Large piece of tag board or cardboard
- Pencil
- Brushes
- Scissors or utility knife
- Spray paint
- Craft paint
- Glue
- Glitter

Cut a sheet of tag board or cardboard with scissors or a utility knife into the shape you want. Spray-paint the background color of your choice if using cardboard.

Using a pencil, draw your design for a national seal using the turkey. Don't forget to add symbols and mottos.

Color your seal with paint. For a bit of shine, glue on some gold or silver glitter.

named as his replacement as the American minister to France, or to another European nation. But Congress snubbed Temple and, through him, Franklin.

One man wrote to Adams that when Franklin saw how Temple was passed over, Franklin "will have no Reason to Suppose that his Conduct is much approved." The new minister to France, however, Thomas Jefferson, admired Franklin greatly. He wrote James Monroe in Congress, "Europe fixes an attentive eye on your reception of Doctor Franklin." This will speak to Europe "as an evidence of the satisfaction or dissatisfaction of America with their Revolution."

Sobbing friends saw the nearly 80-year-old Franklin off as he sailed to England. There he met old friends one last time before embarking on his final voyage across the Atlantic. He also saw William. The meeting ended coldly, with no peace rekindled between father and son.

THE GULF STREAM

❧ FRANKLIN SPENT seven weeks at sea. He booked an extra-large cabin so he'd have room to write and make his observations. For thirty years he had read about whaling ships and talked to sea captains, and he had known that ships traveled faster on some courses than others. During his 1776 voyage he'd tracked the daily air and water temperatures, testing the phenomenon of a warm ocean current called the Gulf Stream.

Franklin believed that the Gulf Stream originated in shallows off the Gulf of Florida. There the warm waters shot through the narrow Straits of Florida. The narrowness of the straits sped up the current, which then flowed into the Atlantic and headed north. This warm Gulf Stream moved faster than the rest of the water.

As the first person to put together all the bits and pieces known about the Gulf Stream, Franklin devised an instrument to measure the water temperature at a depth below 100 feet. He spent the 1785 voyage figuring out

---

The Weather Man

FRANKLIN SPENT decades recording and studying weather. Besides his work with lightning, one of the things he observed was that storms typically moved from west to east. He believed a storm's path could be plotted. Franklin made some of the first weather forecasts and printed them in *Poor Richard: An Almanack*. Franklin also discussed with other scholars the effects on weather of cutting down forests. They believed "cleared land absorbs more heat and melts snow faster."

the location, width, and depth of the Gulf Stream. In 1786 he mapped his conclusions. Two hundred years later, images taken from space showed that Franklin's map very accurately followed the Gulf Stream.

RETURN TO PHILADELPHIA

❦ ON SEPTEMBER 14, 1785, Franklin's ship docked in Philadelphia. The city met him with ringing bells and crowds of well-wishers, an "affectionate Welcome" beyond the old man's expectations. Booming Philadelphia boasted a population of 40,000—

Struck by Lightning!

DURING RENOVATIONS Franklin discovered that his house had been struck by lightning sometime in the past. His 1752 lightning rod, though bent and blackened, had protected his home from damage. After all that time, he wrote to a friend in 1787, "the invention has been of some use to the inventor."

MAKE A BAROMETER

One of the tools Franklin used to study weather was a barometer, first used in the 1600s. The instrument measures air pressure.

MATERIALS

- Large balloon
- Scissors
- Large metal can, such as a coffee can or a wide tomato sauce can
- Large rubber band
- Tape
- Pin or toothpick
- Drinking straw
- Spiral notebook with lined paper
- Pen

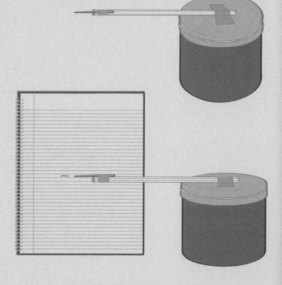

Blow up a balloon; then let the air out. Once it is stretched, cut off a large part of the balloon, as shown.

Stretch the balloon top over the open top of the can. You will need another person to hold the can for you. Stretch a large rubber band around the balloon to hold the balloon tightly in place. It will look like a drum.

Tape a pin or toothpick onto the end of a drinking straw. Lay the straw on top of the balloon and tape it onto the balloon.

Take the barometer outside to a covered spot. A few times a day take a reading from your barometer. Hold the spiral notebook up and see where the pin/toothpick points on the lines. Make a mark.

Make notes about the weather conditions when you check the barometer readings. What do you notice?

What is happening? When air pressure is higher, it pushes on the balloon, making the balloon go down and the straw go upward on the lines on the paper. When the air pressure decreases, the pressure on the balloon is less and the reading will be lower. Usually, low air pressure means rain or clouds. When the barometer drops, a storm may be coming. High pressure usually means clear weather.

tiny when compared with that of London or Paris, but at the time it was the largest city in America. Thanks in large part to Benjamin Franklin's efforts, the city led the nation in arts, medicine, and sciences as well as luxuries such as libraries and paved streets.

Franklin moved into the Market Street house with Sally's growing family of six children, now that Benny had returned. There was an older boy named Willy and "four little prattlers who cling about the knees of their grandpapa and afford him great pleasure," wrote Franklin. Benny enrolled at the school founded by his grandfather, then called the University of the State of Pennsylvania. He graduated in 1787 and became a printer and publisher like his grandfather.

Eventually the house proved too crowded. Franklin had a three-story addition put on: a dining room that seated 24 guests, more

Franklin arrives home and greets Sally and her husband. A sedan chair waits to carry him to his house.

bedrooms, and a library he filled with 4,000 books and assorted musical instruments. The old man enjoyed overseeing the work of numerous carpenters, painters, bricklayers, and stonecutters. Franklin spent his time inventing things, such as a long "grabber" to reach books on high shelves. He read and played cards and cribbage with friends.

Once more, however, Pennsylvania sent Franklin to work in the assembly and as a member of the state's executive council. His desire to help, and to earn the good opinion of his fellow citizens, drove him on even when his body protested it was time to retire. He suffered with gout, painful bladder, and kidney stones, and was often tired. He wrote to a friend in February 1786, "You see that old as I am, I am not yet grown insensible, with respect to Reputation."

Franklin as an old man.

MAKE A WALKING STICK
FOR YOUR GOUT

MATERIALS

Adult supervision required

- Paint or wood stain
- Brushes
- Dowel rod, one inch thick
- Modeling clay that bakes to harden (such as Sculpey)
- Checker or stamp
- Oven
- Glue

Paint your dowel rod a color or stain it with wood stain. Let it dry.

Make a ball out of the modeling clay, two to three inches in diameter. Fit the ball onto the top of the dowel rod. You can leave it round or flatten it a bit. Use a checker or stamp to put a design on the top if you want. Carefully take the ball off the dowel rod. Bake the clay in the oven following the package directions.

After the clay has baked, hardened, and cooled, paint the clay with a design using a fine brush.

After the paint dries, glue the clay ball onto the dowel rod and you have an 18th-century walking stick!

SLAVERY

Even with all the accomplishments of his long life Franklin hoped to "finish handsomely." "Being now in the last Act, I begin to cast about for something fit to end with," he wrote to George Whitefield. Franklin's new mission became the abolition of slavery. He had traveled for a lifetime to reach this decision.

Franklin had grown up in a world that accepted slavery without a second thought. He owned and bought slaves for thirty years. He printed notices about runaway slaves and servants and the auction of slaves in the *Pennsylvania Gazette*. Like most white people of the time, Franklin felt that Africans lacked the "natural understanding" to be educated.

One of Franklin's first concerns was not for the enslaved people but how slavery affected the white owners. Since the white people had slaves to do the work, the masters and their families grew weak and "enfeebled." White children, he noted in 1751, turned "disgusted with Labour, and being educated in Idleness, are rendered unfit to get a Living by Industry."

During his tours of the colonies as postmaster, Franklin saw schools for black children organized by Thomas Bray, an Anglican minister. This began changing his thinking about the intelligence of African Americans. The black children were "as quick, their Memory as strong, and their Docility in every Respect equal to that of white Children," he wrote to a member of Bray's church in 1763. "You will wonder perhaps that I should ever doubt it." Ten years later Franklin noted that blacks were held back, not for lack of understanding, "but they have not the Advantage of Education."

Franklin slowly moved to the idea that slavery was an injustice that stained the whole notion of liberty and freedom voiced by America. In 1772 he commented when a British court freed a slave just arrived in London. Britain, he said, congratulated itself on freeing a single slave, while British merchants continued a slave trade "whereby so many hundreds of thousands are dragged into slavery." A year later he wrote that slavery had "so long disgrac'd our Nation and Religion."

Pennsylvania Quakers founded the nation's first abolition society. The state also passed the first laws for the gradual end of slavery. Slave children born after 1780 were freed at age 28. In 1787, Franklin became the president of the Pennsylvania Society for Promoting the Abolition of Slavery and the Relief of Negroes Unlawfully Held in Bondage. How could a person "treated as a brute

An 18th-century antislavery illustration.

animal" know what to do as an ordinary citizen? He supported efforts to aid freed blacks with jobs and education to help them move into society.

"EXPERIMENTS IN POLITICS"

THE SAME year Franklin became president of the Abolition Society, duty called him to a new convention in Philadelphia. The old Articles of Confederation, written during the American Revolution, had run out of steam. Under the Articles, Congress had few powers to govern—it could not coin money, pass taxes, or oversee trade between the states. There was no chief executive or president, no national court system. The states hoarded powers to themselves.

So, should the Articles be preserved so that power remained in the states, or should a new federal government be created, making the United States truly one nation? The delegates decided to scrap the Articles and write a new blueprint of American government.

In May 1787, Pennsylvania sent Franklin as a delegate to the Constitutional Convention in Philadelphia. Ben, age 81, was the oldest delegate. He nominated George Washington for president of the convention. Franklin, with Sally's help, hosted dinners and casual meetings outside under the shade of his mulberry tree. Throughout the hot, sticky summer, delegates gathered in Franklin's yard to informally discuss the great matters before them. One man described Franklin as "a short, fat, trunched old man, in a plain Quaker dress, bald pate, and short white locks." He was "the greatest philosopher of the age… a most extraordinary Man," who told a story "in a style more engaging than anything I ever heard."

Poor health kept Franklin away from the convention on some days. Standing to speak racked his poor old body with pain.

Franklin's Proposals

DELEGATES LISTENED politely to many of Franklin's proposals and then rejected them. These included his idea for a unicameral (or one body) legislature, opening each convention session with a prayer for help and guidance, having an executive council instead of a president, and having officeholders serve without pay.

Franklin did not fear democracy, or rule of the people, as much as most of the men at the convention. He opposed measures requiring a man to own a certain amount of property in order to hold office. He also spoke against property requirements for men to vote. Franklin wrote to a friend in France, "We are making experiments in politics."

Delegates such as Alexander Hamilton discussed matters under Franklin's mulberry tree.

can be made that is not contested; the numerous objections confound the understanding; the wisest must agree to some unreasonable things, that reasonable ones of more consequence may be obtained."

Franklin contributed to the greatest compromise of the convention, which brought the wary large and small states together. There would be two houses of Congress, the Senate and the House of Representatives. Each state, no matter its size, would have two senators with equal votes, a nod to the smaller states. In the House of Representatives, representation would be based on a state's population, a nod to the large states. A bill needed approval of both houses to become law.

Slavery would continue in the United States. The convention voted to end the importation of slaves to the United States, but this was not to go into effect until 1808. For the purpose of representation, each slave would be counted as three-fifths of a person.

In September, Franklin urged his fellow delegates to sign the new Constitution of the United States. "I confess," said Franklin, "that I do not entirely approve this Constitution at present." But, he told the delegates, he doubted that they could have made a better Constitution. "When you assemble a number of men, to have the advantage of their joint wisdom" you also gained "their prejudices,

When he wished to have his views known, he wrote them out and had them read to the convention.

Franklin knew that only compromise could give birth to a new constitution. His efforts to bring the other delegates together often left him exhausted. A year later he explained to a friend in France: "Not a move their passions, their errors of opinion, their local interests, and their selfish views," noted Franklin. "It therefore astonishes me, Sir, to find this system approaching so near to perfection as it does; and I think it will astonish our enemies," who waited for America to fail. "Thus I consent, Sir, to this Constitution because I expect no better, and because I am not sure that it is not the best."

As the delegates left the convention, Elizabeth Powell, the wife of Philadelphia's mayor, caught sight of Franklin.

"Doctor," she called, "what have we got, a republic or a monarch?"

"A republic, madam" replied Franklin, "if you can keep it."

THE CLOSING YEARS

FRANKLIN BEGAN work on the third part of his autobiography in 1788, detailing his work to benefit people and his public service

Unlike this 19th-century illustration, the elderly Franklin rarely stood and spoke at the convention.

A Rising Sun

AS THE delegates stepped forward to sign the Constitution, Franklin mused how he'd often studied the half-sun design on the back of the chair that Washington sat in as president of the convention. He'd not been "able to tell whether it was rising or setting; but now, at length, I have the happiness to know that it is a rising and not a setting sun." And so, Franklin expressed his hopes for the new plan of government.

A close-up of the "rising sun" chair Washington sat in during the Constitutional Convention.

CAST FRANKLIN'S RISING SUN

MATERIALS

Adult supervision required

- Old newspapers
- Play sand
- Disposable foil roasting pan, about 3 inches deep
- Water
- Paint stirrer
- An unsharpened pencil
- Wire cutter
- Chicken wire
- Measuring cup
- Bag of plaster
- Plastic paint bucket
- Wire coat hanger

Spread the newspaper on a table to work on. Add about 2 inches of sand to the foil roasting pan. Dampen the sand with water and stir it around with the paint stirrer. Pat the sand down to be smooth and even.

Using a pencil, trace a rising-sun design into the sand. Make sure the line goes down into the sand about an inch. Make it as fancy or simple as you like. It does not have to match the convention chair.

Cut a piece of chicken wire to fit inside the roasting pan—keep this handy for later. Follow the directions on the plaster packaging to mix the dry plaster with water in the plastic paint bucket. Slowly pour about half of the plaster over the sand, making sure the plaster fills your design in the sand.

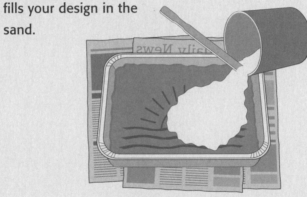

To help support your sand casting, place the chicken wire on top of the plaster. Pour the rest of the plaster over the chicken wire and fill the roasting pan.

Cut a piece of the wire coat hanger and bend it like an upside-down block U, as shown. Put the coat hanger U into the plaster along the top edge. This will let you hang your sand casting.

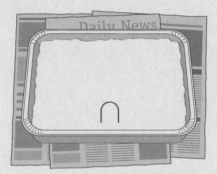

Let the plaster set and dry. When it is completely dried, carefully lift it out of the roasting pan. Brush off the sand or rinse the sand casting with a garden hose; some sand will remain embedded. Your design should show in the plaster. Now—hang your plasterwork up!

up till his arrival in England in 1757. Sometime in the winter of 1789–90, he wrote a fourth section dealing with events of 1758. *The Autobiography of Benjamin Franklin* remains in print today, a gem of American literature.

Franklin returned to his roots in another way, too. He founded the Franklin Society to help printers needing credit or insurance. And he delighted in helping his grandson Benny set up in the family trade.

Franklin also wrote his will. Over the years he'd helped many of his large family, his siblings, his nieces and nephews, and his children. He left his library of 4,000 books, money, and his papers to Temple. Sally received most of her father's estate, with the note that Sally's husband must free his slave. One of Sally's most valuable gifts was a miniature portrait of King Louis XVI circled with diamonds. Franklin requested that Sally not make vain, expensive, and useless jewelry out of the diamonds. He also left money to both Boston and Philadelphia to aid young craftsmen and mechanics who had served an apprenticeship and wanted to start a business.

Franklin signed (and probably wrote) an address to America about ending slavery and educating and employing freed slaves. In February 1790, Franklin signed a petition urging the new Congress to grant "liberty to those unhappy men who alone in this land of freedom are degraded in perpetual bondage." The petition challenged the notion that Congress should do nothing about the slave trade until 1808, as written in the Constitution.

The petitions from the Quaker societies unleashed angry debates in Congress. A congressman from South Carolina questioned Franklin's support for the abolition of slaves, exclaiming, "Even great men have their senile moments." A congressman from Pennsylvania rushed to Franklin's defense. Franklin's views on slavery rose from the "qualities of his soul, as well as those of his mind" and Franklin still could "speak the language of America, and … call us back to our first principles." But the antislavery petitions died in Congress.

By the spring of 1790, Franklin knew his days were numbered. Gout, kidney stones, lung problems, and a sprained wrist that would not heal plagued his once-energetic body. He spent his time reading. He wrote to a friend that his life had seen him rise from "small and low beginnings to such high rank." The pricks and pains of old age were a means of weaning him from a world where "he was no longer fit to act the part assigned to him."

He wrote letters of farewell, including one to the new president, George Washington. Out of all other Americans, perhaps only the president could understand the great fame thrust upon Franklin, for the same thing had happened to Washington.

For my own personal Ease I should have died two Years ago, but tho' these Years have been spent in excruciating Pain, I am pleas'd that I have liv'd them, since they have brought me to our present Situation. I am now finishing my 84th year, and probably with it my career in this Life; but in whatever state of Existence I am plac'd hereafter, if I retain any Memory of what has pass'd here, I shall with it retain the Esteem, Respect, and Affection with which I have long been, my dear Friend, Yours most sincerely, B. Franklin.

Early in April, Franklin caught a fever. His breathing grew labored and a heavy cough tormented him. Opium relieved some of the pain. Family and friends gathered close at hand—Sally and her husband, his grandchildren, and even Polly Stevenson, who'd moved to Philadelphia with her family. As her father weakened, Sally whispered she wished he'd get better and live many more years. "I don't," replied Franklin. At the end an abscess burst in his lung and he could no longer speak. He held Benny's hand. At 11 P.M. on April 17, 1790, Franklin died with his family at his bedside. He was 84 years old.

Crowds of 20,000 people jammed Philadelphia's streets to mourn Franklin and witness the funeral procession to Christ Church's burial grounds. Meanwhile, tributes poured in from France. One Frenchman called Franklin "this mighty genius" who'd spread the rights of man throughout the world, a man "able to conquer both thunderbolts and tyrants." The French National Assembly declared three days of national mourning for Franklin.

Franklin was the unschooled genius, brilliant and probing, who took Europe by storm. Franklin, who met with kings, held dear his common touch. He was the inventor, the scientist, the curious man who never stopped marveling at the natural world around him. He was a writer, an editor, and a publisher who used his gifted pen to bring change, challenge falsehoods, encourage others, and entertain. Money and power meant nothing to him if they were not used to better people's lives. There was Franklin the man of compromise, the man who believed a solution could always be found. This Franklin sought solutions as an assemblyman, a commissioner, and a delegate to conventions. Most of all there was Franklin the diplomat, who kept the French alliance—and America's hopes of independence—alive based solely on his personality, understanding, and skill.

PHILADELPHIA, 22 April.
The following was the order of Proceſſion yeſterday at the funeral of our late learned and illuſtrious citizen, Dr. FRANKLIN.
All the Clergy of the city, before the corpſe.
THE CORPSE,
Carried by Citizens.
The Pall ſupported by The Preſident of the State, the Chief Juſtice—the Preſident of the Bank, Samuel Powell, William Bingham, and David Rittenhouſe, Eſquires,
Mourners,
Conſiſting of the family of the deceaſed—with a number of particular friends,
The Secretary and Members of the Supreme Executive Council.
The Speaker and Members of the General Aſſembly.
Judges of the Supreme Court,
And other Officers of Government.
The Gentlemen of the Bar.
The Mayor and Corporation of the city of Philadelphia.
The Printers of the city, with their Journeymen and Apprentices.
The Philoſophical Society.
The College of Phyſicians.
The Cincinnati.
The College of Philadelphia.
Sundry other Societies—together with a numerous and reſpectable body of Citizens.
The concourſe of ſpectators was greater than ever was known on a like occaſion. It is computed that not leſs than 20,000 perſons attended and witneſſed the funeral. The order and ſilence which prevailed, during the Proceſſion, deeply evinced the heartfelt ſenſe, entertained by all claſſes of citizens, of the unparralleled virtues, talents, and ſervices of the deceaſed.

The order of Franklin's funeral procession from the *Gazetteer of the United States.*

A month before Franklin's death, Ezra Stiles, a friend, a clergyman, and president of Yale University, asked Franklin for his religious views. Franklin wrote back that he believed in God, the "Creator of the Universe. That he governs it by his Providence. That he ought to be worshipped. That the most acceptable Service we render him is doing good to his other children." He confessed that while he tried to follow Jesus' teachings, he wasn't sure about the divinity of Jesus. He had not studied about Jesus "and think it needless to busy myself with now, when I expect soon an opportunity of knowing the truth with less trouble."

In a 1785 letter to George Whatley, Franklin, always practical, observed that in nature nothing is wasted, "not even a Drop of Water." He could not believe that God would "suffer the daily Waste of Millions of Minds ready made that now exist, and put himself to the continual Trouble of making new ones." Franklin did not see an end in death, but a new beginning. "Thus finding myself to exist in the World," he wrote to Whatley, "I believe I shall, in some Shape or other, always exist." He hoped the mistakes of his past life would be corrected in the new.

As a young man in 1728, Franklin had written an epitaph:

The body of
B. Franklin, Printer
(Like the Cover of an Old Book
Its Contents torn Out
And Stript of its Lettering and Gilding)
Lies Here, Food for Worms.
But the Work shall not be Lost;
For it will (as he Believ'd) Appear once
  More
In a New and More Elegant Edition
Revised and Corrected
By the Author.

But at the end, Franklin made only a simple request: a marble slab six feet long and four feet wide, without ornament, to cover his grave. The only inscription—"Benjamin and Deborah Franklin: 1790"—carved across the marble's face.

GLOSSARY

Assembly: the legislature of a state or colony

Contagion: a disease caught by direct or indirect contact

Convex: a surface, like the lens on Franklin's spectacles, that curves or rounds outward

Copperplate: a flat piece of copper used for printing or etching

Deism: belief in God based on evidence of reason and nature; belief that God created the Universe, then left it alone, not intervening in events

Empiricism: a method of experimenting, searching for knowledge based on observation

Epitaph: an inscription on a tomb or monument, a poem or writing praising the deceased person or, in Mungo's case, the deceased squirrel

Equilibrium: a state of balance due to the equal action of opposing forces

Frugal/Frugality: spending little, watching your money carefully

Legislature: an organized body of people empowered to make laws

Militia: citizens who practice military maneuvers part-time and are called to action during an emergency, after which they go home

Parliament: the supreme legislative body of Great Britain; made up of the House of Lords and the House of Commons

Privateer: an armed ship privately owned and manned that is authorized by a government during wartime to attack and capture enemy ships

Reconcile/Reconciliation: to settle a quarrel or dispute; to bring into harmony or agreement

Republic: a type of democracy in which the people have power through their elected representatives

Salon: a popular 18th-century gathering of guests that included leaders in society, politics, sciences, and the arts

Satire: writing that exposes or denounces human vices or folly through wit, scorn, sarcasm, and irony

PLACES TO VISIT AND WEB RESOURCES

Benjamin Franklin Institute of Technology
See the original color paintings of the Charles Mills Murals in the Union Building.
41 Berkeley Street
Boston, Massachusetts 02116

Chateau de Versailles
Take a virtual tour of the dazzling Palace of Versailles, where Franklin served as a diplomat to the court of King Louis XVI.
www.chateaudeversailles.fr/fr/

Christ Church Burial Ground
See Franklin's grave and other "founding fathers."
Fifth and Arch Streets
Philadelphia, Pennsylvania 19106
www.oldchristchurch.org

Franklin Court
Site of Franklin's house, with a museum that includes a glass armonica.
318 Market Street
Philadelphia, Pennsylvania 19106
(215) 965-2305
www.nps.gov/inde

Franklin's Print Shop
Visit a working 18th-century print shop in action.
320 Market Street
Philadelphia, Pennsylvania 19106
(215) 965-2305
www.nps.gov/inde/

Independence National Historical Park
See where the Declaration of Independence and the Constitution were born. See the "rising sun" chair and the Liberty Bell.
143 S. Third Street
Philadelphia, Pennsylvania 19106
(800) 537-7676
www.nps.gov/inde/

JOIN, or DIE.

Museum of the American Philosophical Society

Founded by Franklin in 1743. Visit the museum that houses many of Franklin's papers.
104 S. Fifth Street
Philadelphia, Pennsylvania 19106
(215) 599-4283
www.amphilsoc.org

National Constitution Center

See life-size bronze statues of all the signers and one of the original copies of the Constitution.
525 Arch Street
Philadelphia, Pennsylvania 19106
(215) 409-6700
www.constitutioncenter.org

The Benjamin Franklin House

The only surviving Franklin home, today a museum, is his Craven Street residence in London. Take a virtual tour.
36 Craven Street, London, England
www.benjaminfranklinhouse.org

The Franklin

A hands-on interactive museum.
222 N. 20th Street
Philadelphia, Pennsylvania 19103
(215) 448-1200
www.fi.edu

FURTHER READING FOR KIDS

Fleming, Candace. *Ben Franklin's Almanac.* New York: Atheneum, 2003.

Fleming, Thomas. *Benjamin Franklin: Inventing America.* New York: Sterling, 2007 reprint.

Fradin, Dennis Brindell. *Who Was Benjamin Franklin?* New York: Grosset and Dunlap, 2002.

Herbert, Janis. *The American Revolution for Kids: A History with 21 Activities.* Chicago: Chicago Review Press, 2002.

Hollihan, Kerrie L. *Isaac Newton and Physics for Kids: His Life and Ideas with 21 Activities.* Chicago: Chicago Review Press, 2009.

Miller, Brandon Marie. *Declaring Independence: Life During the American Revolution,* Minneapolis: Lerner Publishing, 2005.

Miller, Brandon Marie. *George Washington for Kids: His Life and Times.* Chicago: Chicago Review Press, 2007.

Roop, Peter, and Connie Roop. *Benjamin Franklin.* New York: Scholastic Reference, 2001.

SELECTED RESOURCES

Dray, Phillip. *Stealing God's Thunder: Benjamin Franklin's Lightning Rod and the Invention of America.* New York: Random House, 2005.

Isaacson, Walter. *Benjamin Franklin: An American Life.* New York: Simon and Schuster, 2003.

Lemay, J. A. Leo, ed. *Benjamin Franklin, Autobiography, Poor Richard, and Later Writings.* New York: Library of America, 2005.

Lopez, Claude-Anne. *The Private Franklin: The Man and His Family.* New York: W. W. Norton, 1985.

Morgan, Edmund. *Benjamin Franklin.* New Haven: Yale University Press, 2003.

Morgan, Edmund, ed. *Not Your Usual Founding Father: Selected Readings from Benjamin Franklin.* New Haven: Yale University Press, 2006.

Rhodehamel, John, ed. *The American Revolution: Writings from the War of Independence.* New York: Library of America, 2001.

Wood, Gordon S. *The Americanization of Benjamin Franklin.* New York: Penguin Press, 2004.

INDEX

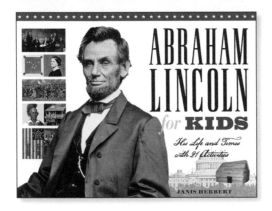

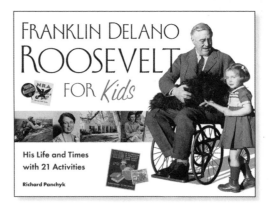

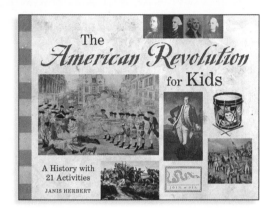

The American Revolution for Kids

A History with 21 Activities
By Janis Herbert
Ages 9 & up
Two-color interior, photos and
illustrations throughout
A Smithsonian Notable Book for Children

"The dramatic events that lay behind the Founding Fathers' struggle for liberty are vividly recounted in Herbert's lively survey."

—*Smithsonian*

The true accounts of those who created the United States come to life in this activity book celebrating freedom and democracy.

ISBN 978-1-55652-456-1
$16.95 (CAN $18.95)

Isaac Newton and Physics for Kids

His Life and Ideas with 21 Activities
By Kerrie Logan Hollihan
Ages 9 & up
Two-color interior, photos and
illustrations throughout

"Hollihan introduces readers to the scientific brilliance, as well as the social isolation, of this giant figure, blending a readable narrative with an attractive format.... [T]his book gives readers a clear picture of Newton's impact on the study of physics and astronomy."

—*Booklist*

ISBN 978-1-55652-778-4
$16.95 (CAN $18.95)